No one knows more about movem[
The Rise and Fall of Movements, Ad
presenting his research on moveme
why they grow and why they declir
you will discover what it takes to sustain movements and why they matter. I highly recommend this book to every church leader, church planter, network leader, and denominational leader.

DAVE FERGUSON, lead pastor of Community Christian Church, Chicago; author of *Hero Maker*

Steve Addison is a blast of fresh air. In *The Rise and Fall of Movements* I find a primer on where I've gone right and where I've gone wrong leading a church multiplication movement. Not just descriptive, he prescribes a return to Jesus as the source of all identity that drives mission, strategy, and methods. This book provides a painful, yet hopeful, path to a better future for the church in the West.

RALPH MOORE, founder of the Hope Chapel movement; church multiplication catalyzer at Exponential

Steve's best yet—I underlined something on every page. Eminently readable because it is also personal, *The Rise and Fall of Movements* is a scholarly look back at what made movements flourish or fail, a practical look at what God is doing right now, and an inspiring look forward to the best that is yet to come.

ANTHONY DELANEY, leader of Ivy Church Network, Manchester, UK; director of NewThing, Europe

Many people talk about movements but few understand them. Steve Addison is an international expert on the topic. *The Rise and Fall of Movements* is a brief study of the birth, life, and death of movements that is informed by biblical truth, personal experience, historical analysis, and contemporary realities. Addison reminds us that kingdom-advancing movements are simple and Spirit-led. This book calls us to keep our identities in Christ and his Word; to keep strategies practical, and methods flexible.

J. D. PAYNE, missiologist and author; associate professor of Christian Ministry, Samford University, Birmingham, Alabama

In this helpful book, Addison has captured which catalytic factors tend to result in Jesus movements and what influences have tended to result in their decline. Though movements tend to come and go, Addison reminds us that if we are faithful to follow Jesus, and fish for people, Jesus will be faithful to use us, ordinary as we may be, to spread his kingdom to the ends of the earth.

GEORGE ROBINSON, associate professor of Evangelism and Missions; Headrick chair of World Missions

Do you want to see multiplying movements? Steve has done the research and provided insights for leaders at each stage. I enjoyed the story and the lessons from the early Methodist movement under Wesley. I was challenged by the factors that cause movements to settle down.

MARCUS ROSE, founder of HOPE; chairman of Vision Hope International

Movements are the way that God has filled the world with the knowledge of himself. When one movement wanes, another waxes. In this latest volume, in a series of his life's works on movements, Addison draws conclusions that answer the "why" questions as well as the "what." Gleaning from the past will help this generation prepare for the future. I've devoured each book that Addison has written, and this one was no exception.

PEYTON JONES, author of *Reaching The Unreached* and *Church Zero*

A needed addition to the evolving literature on movement dynamics.

ALAN HIRSCH, award-winning author; founder of 100Movements, 5Q Collective, and Forge International

Also by Steve Addison

Movements That Change the World:
Five Keys to Spreading the Gospel

What Jesus Started: Joining the Movement,
Changing the World

Pioneering Movements: Leadership That
Multiplies Disciples and Churches

THE
RISE AND FALL
OF
MOVEMENTS

A ROADMAP FOR LEADERS

STEVE ADDISON

100
MOVEMENTS
PUBLISHING

First published in 2019 by 100Movements Publishing

www.100mpublishing.com

ISBN 978-0-9986393-6-9

Proofreading: Helen Bearn
Cover design: Lindy Martin
Interior illustration: Peter Bergmeier
Author photo: Michelle Addison

To Danni, Gretta, Robert, and Lachlan

The grass withers and the flowers fall,
but the word of our God endures forever.

Isaiah 40:8

CONTENTS

FOREWORD

Steve Addison is a prophetic student and analyst of Great Commission movements for today's generation. From his classic *Movements That Change the World* (2009), to the biblically expositional *What Jesus Started* (2012), and the inspirational *Pioneering Movements* (2015), Addison has guided us on a journey of understanding how God is at work in fulfilling his Great Commission.[1]

The twin themes of the Great Commission will always be quality and quantity. Quality speaks to the church as a continuation of the life, teachings, and nature of Jesus who was and is the pioneer and perfecter of our faith. The imperative of quantity is found in Christ's commission to reach all nations and extend his kingdom to the ends of the earth.

Likewise, the twin obstacles to this Great Commission are found in quality and quantity. Quality is threatened by a Christian religion that drifts away from the exemplary life of Jesus. The quantitative challenge appears as global population growth threatens to overwhelm any missionary enterprise that ignores the necessity of church planting movements as God's vehicle for outstripping the world's rampant population growth.

My own research published in *Church Planting Movements* (2004), and *A Wind in the House of Islam* (2014), attest to the ways that God is using movements to power the church forward both qualitatively and quantitatively to fulfill his Great Commission.[2] Sadly, the West has been slow to seize upon these models of advance, resulting in a steady decline in both the qualitative and quantitative presence of Christ's kingdom in the West.

In *The Rise and Fall of Movements*, Steve takes us to a new level of insight providing a roadmap through the birth, growth, maturity, decline, and decay of movements. Drawing from the rich stores of church history, this book helps us to see how brothers and sisters through the ages have experienced the exuberance of movement birth and the sad, but not inevitable, decline and decay of the same. At every stage of these life-cycles, it is a renewed commitment to the life of Jesus that offers hope for a more desirable future.

We have much to learn from the global and historic body of Christ, and Steve Addison has ranged far and wide to mine from our under-tapped legacy the lessons that we can, and must, apply if we are to find our place in God's global design for the nations.

The unveiled secret to all movements is found in Addison's clear and unmistakable observation that "at every stage, the way forward begins with returning to Jesus, the apostle and pioneer of our faith."

It is my prayer that God will use this powerful resource to

return us all to that central message, and in so doing, we will see a rebirth of the movements that God will use to draw the very ends of the earth to the kingdom of his Son.

David Garrison
Executive director, Global Gates

THE BEGINNING

Thirty years ago my wife, Michelle, and I planted our first church in the outer suburbs of Melbourne. We had a good sending church behind us and a strong team. The first Sunday, over one hundred people showed up. For the next eighteen months we added an average of one new family to the church every week.

I was a successful church planter—at least in my mind. Then we walked into the middle of a church fight. I was shaken to the core and began seeking God in prayer and in the Scriptures. It wasn't discipline; it was desperation. Early each day I would stoke up the wood burner in my garage, open my Bible and my heart. That garage became holy ground. Through that painful experience God got my attention. I had been caught up in *my* ministry and the growth of *my* church, but God wanted to work on my identity in Christ and to prepare me for a much greater challenge than planting just one church. I discovered for the first time that God had movements on his heart; movements of disciples and churches—everywhere.

I emerged from that experience a different person: I had found my calling, or rather, my calling had found me. God had reshaped my identity in the wilderness. I'm glad he didn't tell me at the time that there would be many more wilderness experiences. I thought one was enough! It seems God is preoccupied with helping us discover our true identity in him.

Twelve months later, Michelle and I left the church plant in good hands and stepped out to plant again, this time by pioneering with just a small team in the inner city and just a few financial supporters. Half the week I was in the harvest, the other half I was pushing a wheelbarrow. I'm an introvert with no desire to meet new people, so every day I would dread the prospect of going out to share Christ. Yet I would return every time amazed that God had led us to prepared people.

Looking back, God was continuing to chip away at what I will describe later as my *Identity*. He was calling me to fuel multiplying movements with a small team, while working as a builder's laborer, raising a young family, and facing financial crises most weeks.

Throughout this time, I was a voracious reader of historical and contemporary movement case studies. I wanted to understand what made them tick. Why did they rise and fall? I read everything I could get my hands on: biblical material, church history, sociology, organizational dynamics, biographies. Through my research I began to identify recurring patterns and characteristics of movements throughout their lifecycle. I drafted two books, one on the characteristics of dynamic movements, which later became my first book, *Movements That Change the World*, and a second, which has become this book, on the rise and fall of movements.

So God was training my head, my heart, and my hands in movement dynamics.

Fast forward to 2008: I've been on this journey for twenty years, training church planters, coaching church planters, advising denominations on their church planting strategies. Churches are being planted, but we're not even close to multiplying movements. Most of my life I've faced recurring bouts of depression. Normally I managed, but this was the big one; my life ground to a halt for about six months and I could barely function. I felt like all my dreams had faded. I was sitting in my psychiatrist's office and told him, "I feel like my life is over. It has no purpose. I'll leave no legacy." He pulled out a Bible from his desk draw, opened it and began reading verses on the love of God. Then he looked me in the eye and said, "Who promised a legacy? Who promised that your dreams would be fulfilled? The only guarantee you have is the unconditional love of God!"

A week later I was walking beside the creek that runs by the end of our street. I thought, "I could wake up every day for the rest of my life feeling just like this. My hopes and dreams dashed without knowing why." Then I thought, "What do I have left? I have Jesus who died for me and rose from the dead. I have the unconditional love of God for all eternity." Then I thought, "Ok, if that's the deal I'll take it."

There was a diabolical side to this battle. God was at work, but so was Satan. He saw his opportunity to destroy my life, my ministry, my relationships. I discovered the greatest weapon of all in the spiritual battle: I laid down my dreams and, broken, I entrusted my life to God (James 4:7). When I was at my weakest, God was shaping my Identity. In the desert, his Spirit was conforming me to the image of his Son. I feel like I died that day, and then God gave me my life back again—as a gift. He gave me back everything I felt I had lost, but now *he* mattered more to me than his gifts.

God had brought me back to the importance of Identity. After twenty years of research and practice, I was also clear about what I will describe later as movement *Strategy*. But there was still a missing piece to this puzzle. I'd taught hundreds of leaders around the world on the characteristics of movements, I'd trained church planters, pastors and denominational teams on implementation. Churches were planted but where was the fruit? We weren't seeing multiplying disciples and churches.

That's when I realized everyone I trained learned movement principles, but they didn't know what to do on Monday morning. The principles were right, but they have to be grounded in action, and action has to be informed by best practice. Enter Jeff Sundell, recently returned to the United States from ten years in India and Nepal. Jeff understood movements as a practitioner, trainer, and coach. He'd seen movements in South Asia and now he was applying the learning in a Western setting. As he met others on the same journey, a coalition formed which is now known as NoPlaceLeft. So I invited Jeff to come and train us in Australia.

Jeff knew the principles, but he gave us the best practice *Methods* we needed to turn our theory into action. (We'll unpack Methods later.) He taught us the basics of how to connect with people, how to share the gospel, how to make disciples through Discovery Bible Studies, how to form discipleship groups that become churches, and how to multiply leaders. We now knew what to do on Monday morning. (You can read more about NoPlaceLeft current practice in chapter eight and in the appendix.) I learned that *Identity* and *Strategy* must be translated into action using best practice *Methods*. Without action, *Identity* and *Strategy* remain untested, abstract concepts.

Now the pieces fit together—Identity, Strategy, Methods. A thirty-year journey and I end up back where it began, with the ministry of Jesus, and the movement he started. It's the movement he continues to lead through his Word and the Holy Spirit, until his Mission is completed, and all things are surrendered to his rule when he hands over the kingdom to the Father, so that God is all in all (1 Corinthians 15:24–28).

We live in troubled times. Is there any age since the time of Christ when that statement was not true? I don't think so. Jesus promised his followers trouble. He promised persecution. He promised natural disasters and war. Not just at the very end of history but throughout it. We aren't home yet, and there's a job to do.

This is Luke's account of what happened when the risen Lord Jesus appeared to his fearful, doubting, troubled disciples.

Notice how Jesus' final instructions are built around his understanding of the Word, the Holy Spirit, and the Mission.

> *Then he opened their minds so they could understand the Scriptures [Word]. He told them, "This is what is written: The Messiah will suffer and rise from the dead on the third day, and repentance for the forgiveness of sins will be preached in his name to all nations, beginning at Jerusalem [Mission]. You are witnesses of these things. I am going to send you what my Father has promised; but stay in the city until you have been clothed with power from on high [Spirit]."*
>
> LUKE 24:45–49

Notice how clear this is. Realize this mandate was not just given to a select few but to *every disciple.*

We are no less fearful, doubting, or troubled than these first disciples. Yet God has chosen the despised and weak things of this world to shame the wise. He has chosen you as a partner in this great cause. The risen Lord has given you the authority to make disciples of the nations; he has equipped you for this Mission with his mighty Word and his Holy Spirit. He has promised to go with you.

This is a book for people who want to go on that journey with him.

INTRODUCTION

Never in so short a time has any ... set of ideas, religious,
political, or economic, without the aid of physical force or
of social or cultural prestige, achieved so commanding a
position in such an important culture.
—Kenneth Scott Latourette

Jesus founded a missionary movement with a mandate to make disciples of the nations. As the risen Lord he still leads the way through his Word and the Holy Spirit. A movement is a group of people committed to a common cause. There is a difference between a ministry and a movement. A ministry is what you can achieve helped by others. The vision is limited to your sphere of control. A movement mobilizes people to act without your direct supervision. Once that happens, the movement is on its way to becoming a great-grandparent— trusting God to give generations of descendants.

For good or for ill, movements are the driving force of history, and history is the story of the rise and fall of movements. So how can a movement, founded by Jesus, not only rise but fall? And if it falls, what hope is there for new life? This is a book about how movements rise and fall and how they are renewed. It is a roadmap for leaders to understand and appreciate the movement lifecycle and how they can navigate their way through it, leading others faithfully in the example Jesus set.

The story begins three centuries after the time of Christ with the movement he founded at the height of worldly success.

NICAEA, AD 325

The Emperor Constantine, robed in purple and adorned with jewels, entered and sat down on a chair of gold. Two hundred and fifty Christian leaders rose to their feet. As he looked out on the bishops he had assembled, Constantine saw empty eye sockets and mutilated limbs, grotesque reminders of the past. These men had been tortured by the empire he now represented. But after three centuries, Rome's fury was spent. Persecution had failed to crush the movement that began with Jesus.

This missionary movement—founded by a crucified criminal in an insignificant province—was everywhere. In an empire of sixty million people, one in ten called Jesus of Nazareth "Lord." Christianity was the most tight-knit and widespread organization in the most powerful empire on earth. These leaders represented the churches of North Africa, Europe, and the East as far as Persia.

The Council of Nicaea in AD 325 was the first worldwide gathering of Christian leaders. This was Constantine's Council. He had summoned the participants. He had paid their expenses. He enforced the Council's decisions, and any bishop who disagreed faced exile. An empire united under Constantine required a united faith.

Constantine's quest for power began twenty years before, when he was a pagan worshipper of the Unconquered Sun. At his father's death, Constantine's troops had proclaimed him emperor. Constantine then pursued and defeated each of his rivals for power. Before his last major battle outside Rome, Constantine had a vision of the Christian cross, superimposed upon the sun. Above the cross he saw the words, "In this sign you will conquer." Inspired by the vision, Constantine ordered his troops to mark their shields with the sign of the cross. When his enemy Maxentius led his army out from behind Rome's walls, Constantine's troops drove them into the Tiber River, drowning both men and horses. Convinced that the Christian God had given him victory, Constantine determined to serve this God. He put an end to the persecution of Christians and gave Christianity full legal recognition and preference over the pagan gods of Rome.

Under Constantine, Christian values shaped society. The gladiatorial games were no longer funded by the state, and criminals were no longer condemned to die in the arena. Constantine outlawed the branding of prisoners on the face, based on the principle that God made man in his image. Churches became places where slaves could be legally freed. Money flowed from the emperor, through his bishops, to aid the sick, the old, and the destitute. Unwanted babies could not be abandoned to die in the wild. Adultery was outlawed. Sunday became a day of rest.[1] Instead of building pagan temples, Constantine built magnificent churches. The original St. Peter's Basilica in Rome was modeled on an imperial throne hall. The emperor gave the Bishop of Rome an imperial residence and the church received large land holdings.[2]

But Constantine's conversion proved to be a mixed blessing for the Christian movement. Imperial favor transformed the church into "an elite organization, lavishly funded by the state bestowing wealth and power on the clergy."[3] Constantine exempted the clergy from taxation and military service, and he gave bishops judicial power. The rich sons of the aristocracy rushed to fill the growing ranks of the priesthood. With enough money and influence, anyone could buy his way to becoming a bishop. The emperor ruled over the life of the church. The sword of state protected the true faith from heretics, whose writings were destroyed and their church property confiscated. A missionary movement became a state religion at peace with the world.

What a stark contrast to the movement Jesus founded. His followers, energized by the Holy Spirit, took the message of salvation to the world, as Christianity spread through ties of family and friends. Apostolic pioneers linked the networks of congregations which were run by local volunteers.[4] The new faith spread along the trade routes that connected major cities and then into the countryside. The world's first missionary movement knew no bounds of geography, race, or class. Despite violent opposition, by AD 300, the movement had around six million followers.[5] Christianity triumphed before the rise of Constantine. Therefore, whoever wanted to be the Roman emperor had to make peace with this upstart movement.[6]

"Success" changed Christianity. It ceased to be a missionary movement. The church lost interest in evangelizing the barbarians beyond the borders of civilization. Within the empire, coercion replaced persuasion as the method of evangelism. Now the church grew dramatically because of its favored position in society. By the end of the fourth century, the vast majority of people within the empire identified as Christian. Pagan shrines were abolished, and bishops took over government functions. Empire and church were one. The persecuted church became the church of power.

Meanwhile, in the desert caves of Egypt, God was up to something new—a rebirth of the Christian faith in a fresh movement. As Christians in the cities of the Roman Empire lost their fervency, individuals retreated into the desert to seek God alone. While the Council of Nicaea met, a former soldier named Pachomius was organizing isolated desert monks into monastic communities. The monastic movement was born and became the driving force of Christian missions for the next 1500 years.

LEADING THROUGH THE LIFECYCLE

Here is the pattern of church history. Movements are born, and those that survive infancy become growing adolescents. They reach adulthood and survey their achievements. They become complacent and settle down. Some find the will to return to their youthful zeal. Most play it safe and decline. Declining institutions can linger for generations, slowly decaying. Meanwhile, always on the fringe, a new movement is born.

Movement Lifecycle

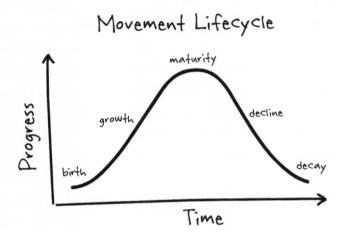

The lifecycle of movements can be broken into five stages—Birth, Growth, Maturity, Decline, and Decay. This process is not inevitable. There is a sixth possibility—the hope of Rebirth during Maturity or Decline. Rebirth interrupts the aging process and turns the movement back towards Growth. In a fallen world Maturity and Decline are predictable; Rebirth goes against the grain. The movement lifecycle is a pattern that shows up over long periods of time. Most movements don't make it past Birth; some movements experience exponential growth for just a few years, others for decades. The lifecycle is a model, and therefore is an abstraction of reality. Models aren't perfect but they do help us navigate complexity.

This book will help you navigate the movement lifecycle. What are the unique challenges and perils at each stage? What kind of leadership is required? You may be pioneering on the edge. You may be riding a wave of expansion. You may be at the peak of success, tempted to play it safe. You may be stuck in suffocating decline, wondering how to turn things around. You need to know where you are on the lifecycle and align yourself with God's purposes revealed in Jesus Christ. We know how Jesus founded and led an expanding missionary movement. We know how he dealt with declining and decaying religious institutions. We know how the risen Lord in Acts intervened and brought correction when that movement stalled. We know how, throughout the biblical story, God renews his people in Mission through his Word and the Holy Spirit.

WHAT'S DRIVING THE RISE AND FALL?

Once we've identified the stages in the movement lifecycle, we need to understand what is driving the process. Why do movements rise and fall? How do we add momentum to the rise, and turn the decline around?

A movement is defined by its Identity. Strategy and Methods are an expression of that Identity. As we look at the ministry of Jesus and other case studies, we'll see how that Identity is the key to the rise and fall of movements.

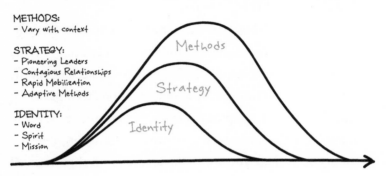

1. Identity—Why?

When I was first drawn to the study of movements, I watched what they did, I discovered characteristics, and I observed Strategies and Methods. Years later I realized I was missing the most important thing: beneath the surface of observable activity is the *why*—Identity. In the next chapter we will see how Jesus lived and ministered out of his Identity as the much-loved Son—obedient to his Father's *Word*, dependent on the *Holy Spirit*, pursuing his *Mission*. Jesus knew *why* he did what he did. His actions sprang from who he was.[7] When Jesus walked out of the wilderness and returned to Galilee in the power of the Spirit, he knew who he was, and he knew what he had come to do.

2. Strategy—How?

Jesus didn't remain alone in the wilderness. He returned to Galilee in the power of the Spirit to launch a missionary movement. He expressed his Identity in strategic action. Strategy is *how* a movement operates. Strategy applies principles in pursuit of the mission. We will learn in chapter one that Jesus' strategy had four recurring aspects: Pioneering Leaders, Contagious Relationships, Rapid Mobilization, and Adaptive Methods. Multiplying movements typically display these patterns.

Strategy must be grounded in Identity—our *how* must serve our why. It is possible to miss the importance of Identity (Word, Spirit, Mission) and view Strategy as the determining factor in movements. We apply the principles to get the results. We build the Tower of Babel to reach the heavens. But God has a way of tearing down our constructions and confusing our efforts to bring us back to the question of Identity.

3. Methods—What?

Strategy is a movement's overarching *how*. Methods are what we do. Methods apply Strategy and they vary according to the context. They are the specific tools, systems, and processes we use to implement Strategy.

Our Methods put flesh on Identity and Strategy, but in the real world they are not always effective. We must continually evaluate our Methods, just as we need to make sure that our Methods align with the other elements of Identity and Strategy.

This is not just a book about better Methods, although we'll discover some along the way. This is a book about aligning who we are (Identity) with the most effective ways (Strategy) to multiply faithful, loving, obedient disciples, and healthy reproducing churches everywhere.

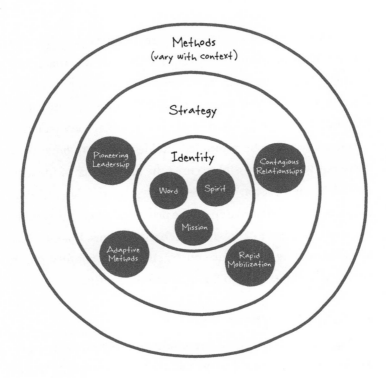

A DIFFERENT WAY OF SEEING THE WORLD

Do we really want to fill this world with the knowledge of Christ? Movements are the only way to achieve that goal. You alone, your church alone, will never fulfill the Great Commission. It takes movements, and movements require a different way of seeing the world.

Think about your church—it may be twenty-five people or 5,000 people. It wouldn't exist without the people and churches that helped get it started. Your church is the fruit of other people and churches whose names may have been long forgotten. Has your church started other churches, or did history stop with you? The Christian faith is a movement that is greater than any one church or ministry. Churches and ministries must serve a greater cause than themselves. One church alone can't fully reach its own community, let alone its city or nation or the nations. A ministry mindset focuses on what we're doing (*our* worship services, *our* youth ministry, *our* online presence, *our* community ministry), whereas a movement mindset is all about releasing authority and responsibility to the newest disciples who make disciples. A church with a ministry mindset finds it hard to see beyond its own achievements; a church with a movement mindset is not impressed with the numbers in the auditorium, but with generations of new disciples, new workers, new churches.

The mission of Jesus became a missionary movement. The church Jesus founded was a missionary church: its existence and activities were an expression of its missionary calling, and its members were fearlessly determined to win others to faith in Jesus as the crucified and risen Messiah. Their mission field began at home in Jerusalem and Judea, and it extended to the ends of the earth. The goal and purpose of their missionary work was the making of disciples and the creation of communities of disciples—people who turned from their old way of life, put their trust in Jesus, and obeyed his teaching.[8]

The central premise of this book is that at every stage of the movement lifecycle the way forward begins with returning to Jesus, the apostle and pioneer of our faith. His example is foundational. His leadership was centered on obedience to the living Word, dependence on the Holy Spirit, and faithfulness to his Mission. The life of Christ in us is the key to leadership at every stage of the lifecycle. Remaining in him is the key to the rise of movements. Abandoning him is the key to the fall of movements.

The movements lifecycle will become clearer as we examine each stage and their respective case studies: Birth (Franciscans), Growth (Methodists), Maturity (Quakers), Decline (pre-Reformation Catholicism), Decay (Student Christian Movement). These stories will provide lessons and warnings to us as we navigate the movement lifecycle. My prayer is that we will learn from these case studies and come to see the world through movement eyes. Finally, we'll examine a contemporary movement in transition from Birth to Growth: NoPlaceLeft is one of hundreds of movements popping up around the world that are pressing forward to fulfill the Great Commission in this generation.

That's where this book is headed. To begin the journey we first need to go back to the day it all began ...

1. WHY MOVEMENTS RISE AND FALL

Jesus' baptism and wilderness sojourn are not merely the first acts of Jesus' public appearance. They are equally the foundation of his whole ministry. Through them the stage of the ensuing drama is set.

—Ulrich Mauser

There came a day when Jesus walked away from his carpenter's shop and his life in Nazareth. Descending from the Galilean hill country, he joined the crowds and headed into the Judean wilderness.[1] Jews were coming to confess their sins and to be baptized by John, the prophet, who warned them to turn back to God or face God's wrath. Religious leaders, tax collectors, soldiers, and common people came, no longer secure in their identity as descendants of Abraham. By being in their midst, Jesus was identifying with rebellious Israel. In choosing to submit himself in baptism, he showed himself to be the Servant of God, prophesied by Isaiah, who would give his life as a ransom for many.[2] As he rose from the water and prayed, the Spirit descended upon Jesus like a dove, and he heard his Father say, "You are my Son, whom I love; with you I am well pleased" (Luke 3:22). Full of the Spirit, Jesus left the Jordan and was led into the desert, where he faced hunger, loneliness, and temptation. Like the first man and woman in the garden, he had to answer the tempter's question, "Did God really say...?"[3]

Each temptation struck at Jesus' identity and the nature of his mission. First, Satan goaded Jesus to satisfy his hunger by turning stones into bread. God had tested Israel in the wilderness with hunger, to teach them that obeying his Word was the most important thing in life.[4] There would come a time when the crowds, satisfied with the bread that Jesus provided, would try to make Jesus king by force (John 6:15). Jesus walked away from the crowds, from their demands, and from political power as the means of bringing in his kingdom. To this and every temptation, Jesus answered: "It is written!" He would live by every word that came from the mouth of God.

The second temptation had Jesus perched high above the Temple in Jerusalem. Satan dared Jesus to throw himself down and force God to rescue him. Years later, as he hung on the cross, those who passed by mocked him with the same words: "If you are the Son of God...." They couldn't believe that the Messiah wouldn't save himself. Of course, Jesus was perfectly capable of doing so, but instead chose to entrust himself to his Father's love. He would not abandon his mission—to save his people from their sins (Matthew 1:21).

Finally, Satan took Jesus to a high mountain and showed him the kingdoms of the world and all their splendor. Jesus could have it all if he would bow down before Satan and worship. Jesus could win the world through political power—without the cross. Yet in response Jesus thundered, "Away from me, Satan! For it is written: 'Worship the Lord your God, and serve him only'" (Matthew 4:10).

Three times Satan tempted Jesus. Three times Jesus answered, "It is written!"

> *"It is written: 'Man shall not live on bread alone, but on every word that comes from the mouth of God.'"* (Matthew 4:4)

> *"It is also written: 'Do not put the Lord your God to the test.'"* (Matthew 4:7)

> *"Away from me, Satan! For it is written: 'Worship the Lord your God, and serve him only.'"* (Matthew 4:10)

It is written. It is written. It is written. In the crisis of temptation, Jesus placed his life and his Mission under the Word of God. Jesus didn't argue with the devil; his only defense was the revelation of God. Unlike Adam and unlike Israel, Jesus obeyed God's Word. At his baptism, Jesus was revealed as God's Son, and in the wilderness, he showed what that Son-ship meant. This conquering king would fulfil his mission as a suffering servant. And from the very start of his ministry, Jesus modelled dependence on the Holy Spirt, choosing to be led by him into the desert.

The baptism and testing of Jesus mark the boundary between his life in Nazareth and the birth of the new Israel. Everything was on the line. Everything we need to know about the heart of the movement Jesus started lies within these two stories. His baptism and testing reveal his Identity as God's much-loved Son—obedient to his Father's Word, dependent on the Holy Spirit, and true to his Mission. If we are to understand how movements are born, why they rise and fall, and how they are reborn, then we must return to the life and ministry of Jesus. Remaining in him is the key to the rise of movements and abandoning him is the reason movements fall.

It is Identity—the Word, the Spirit, and the Mission—that determines the rise and fall of movements that multiply disciples and churches.

SEVEN CHARACTERISTICS OF MULTIPLYING MOVEMENTS

The Word, the Spirit, and the Mission are the first three of seven characteristics of movements that multiply disciples and churches. There are four more characteristics—built upon that foundation of Identity—that describe the pattern of Jesus' Strategy. From these seven foundational characteristics, we can apply Methods—the practical outworking of Strategy.

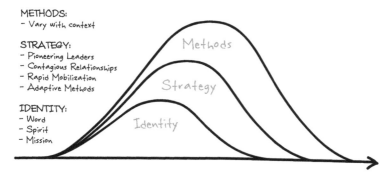

The Rise and Fall of Movements

METHODS:
- Vary with context

STRATEGY:
- Pioneering Leaders
- Contagious Relationships
- Rapid Mobilization
- Adaptive Methods

IDENTITY:
- Word
- Spirit
- Mission

Methods

Strategy

Identity

Identity

1. Word

2. Spirit

3. Mission

Strategy

4. Pioneering Leaders

5. Contagious Relationships

6. Rapid Mobilization

7. Adaptive Methods

IDENTITY

As I've already noted, *Identity* is at the heart of the rise and fall of movements. Jesus' baptism and wilderness experiences are foundational, revealing his Identity as a movement founder. He was obedient to the living Word, dependent on the Holy

Spirit, and faithful to God's Mission. Let's take a look at each of these three components in more detail.

1. Word—obedient to the Word

Jesus placed his life and ministry under the authority of God's living Word—he was the Son who expressed his love in complete obedience. God's Word is God in action: he spoke, and his Word flung the universe into existence. Through speech, God creates, sustains, and shapes reality, and when he speaks it is with authority as our Creator and Lord. Yet God speaks to us as one person speaks to another, in ways we can understand. Our response should be to obey him from our heart.[5] God created the first man and woman through his Word, blessing them, and commanding them to fill the earth and subdue it. He also spoke to set a limit on their autonomy. They were not to eat of the fruit of the tree in the middle of the garden of Eden. God spoke with clarity and authority, and he expected them to obey, needing no other reason than his command. Obedience brings blessing, and disobedience, judgment. Adam and Eve chose disobedience and placed themselves above God's Word. Humans have perpetuated this pattern of placing themselves above God's Word ever since.

In Jesus, the Word became flesh and lived among us, as both perfect God and perfect man. In his earthly ministry, he spoke what his Father taught him (John 8:28; 10:18; 12:49–50; 14:10; 15:15) and his words were God's words. He lived in surrender to the Father's will, obeying the Father's words

(John 5:36; 8:42) and doing nothing in his own authority. Jesus obeyed both the Father's direct commands and the written words of God in the Old Testament. He acted and spoke to fulfill the Scriptures, telling the Pharisees that the Old Testament bore witness to him (John 5:39). At times, Jesus broke with Jewish traditions and interpretations of Scripture, yet he treated the Old Testament as the authoritative word of God, saying, "Do not think that I have come to abolish the Law or the Prophets; I have not come to abolish them but to fulfill them" (Matthew 5:17).

Jesus expected his disciples to follow his example, and stated that to love God is to hear his Word and obey it (John 14:21). Likewise, he told a crowd of his disciples, "My mother and brothers are those who hear God's word and put it into practice" (Luke 8:21). A disciple is simply someone who learns to obey everything Jesus commanded (Matthew 28:20); those who hear his words and obey them are like the wise man who builds his house on rock rather than sand (Matthew 7:24–27).

As the book of Acts unfolds, Luke reports on the spread of God's dynamic Word.[6] The Word spreads, increases, multiplies, and grows in power, traveling to the ends of the earth and conquering the world. Wherever the Word goes, the fruit is new disciples and new churches. Luke organizes the book of Acts around six summary statements. At the heart of God's mission in Acts is the spread of his powerful Word resulting in the multiplication of disciples and churches.[7]

These six summary statements show how Acts is the story of the unstoppable spread of the Word resulting in disciples and churches.

6:7 So the word of God spread. The number of disciples in Jerusalem increased rapidly, and a large number of priests became obedient to the faith.

9:31 Then the church throughout Judea, Galilee and Samaria enjoyed a time of peace and was strengthened. Living in the fear of the Lord and encouraged by the Holy Spirit, it increased in numbers (ESV "it multiplied").

12:24 But the word of God continued to spread and flourish.

16:5 So the churches were strengthened in the faith and grew daily in numbers.

19:20 In this way the word of the Lord spread widely and grew in power.

28:30-31 For two whole years Paul stayed there in his own rented house and welcomed all who came to see him. He proclaimed the kingdom of God and taught about the Lord Jesus Christ—with all boldness and without hindrance!

In Luke's account, the disciples face threats, beatings, jail—even death. Despite these, the Word of God continues to advance. Wherever the Word is met with faith and obedience, the world is turned "upside down" (Acts 17:6, ESV). Households believe, thousands are converted, cities are in uproar, vast regions are reached, and communities of disciples are formed.

At the end of Acts, Paul is in custody in Rome, yet the Word is unstoppable (Acts 28:30–31). Acts' ending shows that the Word will continue to progress. While the recorded account ends, the missionary expansion does not. Despite the obstacles and the suffering, the Word will continue to grow, spread, and multiply.[8]

2. Spirit—dependent on the Holy Spirit

God created all things through his Word and his Spirit. The first man had life through the breath of God. Throughout Israel's turbulent history, God sent deliverers and messengers empowered by the Spirit to restore his people. One day God would send his servant, anointed by the Spirit, to bring salvation to Israel and the whole world (Isaiah 42).

The same Spirit who hovered over the waters at creation was the agent of Jesus' conception. The Spirit who inspired Moses and the prophets filled the witnesses who prophesied about the birth of the Messiah—John (in his mother's womb), Elizabeth, Mary, Zechariah, Simeon, and Anna. To be filled with the Spirit is to bear witness to Jesus.[9] The Spirit watched over Jesus' development from childhood as he grew "in wisdom and stature, and in favor with God and man" (Luke 2:52). At his baptism, the Spirit descended on Jesus as he was praying (Luke 3:21), anointing him with power and authority to fulfill his mission. Jesus, filled with the Spirit, overcame Satan in the wilderness and returned in the power of the Spirit to launch his ministry. "God anointed Jesus of Nazareth with the Holy Spirit and power, and [...] he went around doing good and healing all who were under the power of the devil" (Acts 10:38). From his conception to his ascension, the Holy Spirit was the key to the powerful ministry of Jesus of Nazareth.

Without the Spirit, there would be no missionary movement. Jesus told his disciples it was good he was going away (John 16:7) and that the Father would send the Holy Spirit, so every disciple would know the reality of the presence of God. The disciples were told that the Spirit would guide them into all truth, not speaking on his own but "speaking only what he hears" (John 16:13–14). As the Father sent him, Jesus sent his disciples, knowing that his presence through the Holy Spirit went with them (John 20:21–22).

Jesus' crucifixion, resurrection, and ascension opened the way for the universal outpouring of the Holy Spirit at Pentecost. The Spirit came to enable every believer to bear witness to Jesus (Acts 1:8) and gave wisdom, joy, faith, strength, and courage to the early disciples, in the face of death. The Holy Spirit was at work in major breakthroughs; from Philip's encounter with the Ethiopian eunuch, to Peter's meeting with Cornelius, to Paul and Barnabas's first missionary journey—all were initiated by the Holy Spirit. Blocking Paul from entering Asia Minor and compelling him to go to Jerusalem, the Holy Spirit guided and led the early church. Likewise, the Spirit was behind the appointment of church leaders and the major decisions they made.

The movement Jesus started was a work of God, propelled by the power of the Holy Spirit. As Harry Boer wrote, "Restlessly the Spirit drives the church to witness, and continually churches rise out of the witness."[10] When the Spirit came upon Jesus' disciples as they prayed, the church was born, and the Mission began. Jesus was conceived through the Holy Spirit, he carried out his Mission full of the Spirit, and the church came into existence through the power of the Spirit.

3. Mission—faithful to the core missionary task

The Bible doesn't begin with the story of Israel, but with the creation of the world and of humanity made in God's image. God is Lord over everything he has made including humanity. Sin entered the world when the first man and woman chose to doubt God's character and rebel against his rule. Since then, the whole creation has stood under God's judgment. However, judgment is not his final word. The story of the Bible is the story of God's mission to win back a people for himself from every nation, tribe, and tongue. It began with the calling of Abram, and his covenant with Israel, and continued in the sending of Jesus.

When Jesus called his first disciples he gave them a

command—"Come, follow me"—and then a promise—"I will send you out to fish for people" (Mark 1:17). From the very start of his ministry Jesus' intentions were clear. He founded a missionary movement and those who followed him became missionaries. Even now, as the risen Lord, he continues to pursue his Mission through his disciples. Christianity, if it is true to itself, is a missionary movement.

Following his research on mission in the New Testament, Eckhard Schnabel concluded this about the nature of mission:

> *Missionaries establish contact with non-Christians, they proclaim the news of Jesus the Messiah and Savior (proclamation, preaching, teaching, instruction), they lead people to faith in Jesus Christ (conversion, baptism), and they integrate the new believers into the local community of the followers of Jesus (Lord's Supper, transformation of social and moral behavior, charity).*[11]

These priorities are clear in the ministry of Jesus, in his training of the disciples, and in the continuing ministry of the risen Lord through his Word and the Holy Spirit. The spread of the gospel to the ends of the earth, the training of disciples to follow and obey Christ, and the formation of churches are all at the very heart of God's Mission.

When we look at the life of Jesus, what he trained the

disciples to do, and what he continued to do through Paul and the early church, we can observe him:

- **Connecting** with people who were far from God.
- **Sharing** the good news of Jesus' life, death, and resurrection, calling people to repent and be baptized for the forgiveness of their sin and the promise of the Holy Spirit.
- **Training** new disciples to read God's Word together and to learn to obey what Jesus commanded.
- **Gathering** disciples into churches that reproduce.
- **Multiplying** workers who take the gospel to the ends of the earth.[12]

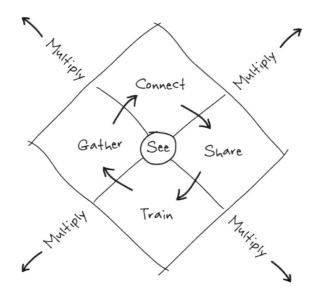

A shift has taken place over the last century in the Western understanding of God's mission and the part we play in it. That shift has resulted in what I call the "missional fog" surrounding Western churches. Increasingly "mission" is framed in political and social terms—fighting for economic justice and world peace, saving the planet, overcoming patriarchy and gender inequality, establishing kingdom businesses, and growing organic vegetables. All these activities and causes have been classified as "mission."[13]

But these are not the core missionary task. Some may be the *fruit* of the gospel, but they are not the gospel itself. This drift from a vertical to horizontal mission has had consequences. Ministries that focus on spreading the gospel, making disciples, and planting churches are no longer a priority. The focus becomes education, relief, and development. The gospel changes everything—inspiring care for the poor, love for the outcast, forgiveness, reconciliation, generosity, sexual purity, and faithfulness in marriage. These are the *overflow* of the gospel in the lives of disciples in community. But they must not be confused with the core missionary task.

The terms *missionary, missions, mission,* and *missional* have become increasingly vague and ill-defined—Westerners have been debating their meaning for the last hundred years. Stephen Neill's prophecy has been fulfilled: "If everything is mission, nothing is mission."[14] Confusion reigns about the gospel and the core missionary task.

Jesus had compassion on the crowds. He fed the hungry

and gave sight to the blind. He freed the captives oppressed by Satan's rule. He preached good news to the humble poor. Yet when the crowds only wanted bread and not the Bread of Life, he identified and challenged their motives (John 6:26–27). There can be no kingdom without the King. There can be no shalom without the Prince of Peace.

We hear a lot about transforming society as the ultimate goal of mission. But is that what Jesus promised us? The people of Nazareth, who knew Jesus best, were the ones who tried to kill him (Luke 4:29). The towns of Chorazin, Bethsaida, and even Capernaum where Jesus spent so much time, were in danger of God's judgment (Matthew 11:21–24). Their inhabitants saw the miracles, they heard the teaching, and yet they would not turn and repent. Even the crowds of Jerusalem called for Jesus' death. Jesus predicted the destruction of Jerusalem and the Temple in AD 70. Jerusalem was not transformed. It was turned upside down. In Acts, cities erupted into riots against the message of the crucified and risen Savior. The gospel was met with fierce resistance in Jerusalem, Arabia, Damascus, Pisidian Antioch, Iconium, Lystra, Philippi, Thessalonica, Berea, Athens, Corinth, Ephesus, and again in Jerusalem.

Paul did not travel to Rome to advise the Emperor Nero on social and foreign policy. He stood before Nero in chains. Eleven of the twelve disciples probably suffered violent deaths. John lived out his years imprisoned on the isle of Patmos. Jesus taught his disciples to expect persecution (Mark 13) and gave no assurance of a transformed world in this age. He promised trouble, saying, "If they persecuted me, they will persecute you also" (John 15:20). Social transformation *can* be a fruit of the gospel, but there is no guarantee it will come.

Jesus' mandate was clear:

> *"All authority in heaven and on earth has been given to me. Therefore go and make disciples of all nations, baptizing them in the name of the Father and of the Son and of the Holy Spirit, and teaching them to obey everything I have commanded you. And surely I am with you always, to the very end of the age."*
>
> MATTHEW 28:18–20

From his position of supreme authority, Jesus gave his followers a universal Mission—make disciples of all peoples. This is the core missionary task. That Mission is supported by the activities of going, baptizing, and teaching others to obey. These activities pick up the force of the central command to "make disciples of all nations." We make disciples of every nation, tribe, and tongue, by going, baptizing, and teaching them to obey everything Jesus has commanded.

There is intention and purpose in our going. Baptism assumes the gospel has been met with repentance, faith, and the gift of the Holy Spirit (Acts 2:38).[15] The Great Commission is not a command to be baptized—it's a command to every disciple to be a baptizer. Teaching is more than passing on information. Disciples are apprentices becoming like their Master; they are those who hear, understand, and obey Jesus' teaching, including faithfulness to the core missionary task. All the nations (*panta ta ethne*) refers not only to nation-states but to every ethnicity, every tribe, and every language, and so the Mission Jesus gives is to make disciples of all people everywhere, without distinction.[16]

The Great Commission ends with a promise: "And surely I am with you always, to the very end of the age." In the Old Testament when Yahweh called his people to a task, he promised to go with them (Exodus 3:12). The Lord makes the same promise to his disciples who obey his Commission—he is present and active on their behalf. In our core mission to make disciples of every people group, the risen Lord promises we will never be alone.

STRATEGY

The four recurring patterns in the Strategy of multiplying movements are found in Jesus' ministry, in his training of the Twelve, and in the mission of Paul and the early church. Each of these elements is covered in depth in my previous books.[17] I'll summarize them here.

4. Pioneering Leaders

As the apostle and pioneer of our faith, Jesus began something new in human history—a global missionary movement. His ministry was mobile; he focused on Israel while preparing workers to go to the nations. The twelve apostles were the bridge that linked Israel and the new people of God. As uniquely authoritative witnesses of the resurrection, they became guardians of the gospel, which was preserved for us in the writings of the New Testament. Another wider group, also known as apostles, shared this call to go into all the world and make disciples. They were pioneer church planters, but they did not share the Twelve's status as authoritative witnesses of the resurrected Lord. Jesus still calls pioneers to lead his people into the fullness of what it means to be a missionary movement.

What do movement pioneers do? They follow the example of Jesus and the disciples he trained:

- **They see the end**. Their Identity is aligned with God's purposes. They submit to the leadership of Jesus through the Holy Spirit and the power of his living Word. They obey God's call to join his Mission.
- **They connect with people.** They cross boundaries (geographic, linguistic, cultural, social, and economic) to establish contact with people far from God.
- **They share the gospel.** They communicate the truth about God and salvation through Christ. They equip new disciples to spread the good news throughout their communities.
- **They train disciples.** They lead people to faith in Jesus Christ (conversion, baptism, gifts of the Holy Spirit) and teach them to obey all that Jesus has commanded.

- **They gather communities.** They form those who repent, believe, and are baptized into churches where they join together to study and obey God's Word, pray, celebrate the Lord's Supper, love one another, worship, give generously, and make disciples (Acts 2:42–47).
- **They multiply workers.** They equip local church leaders to multiply disciples and churches. In partnership with the churches, movement pioneers form apostolic teams that launch into unreached fields.

The history of the Christian movement reveals that breakthroughs in the spread of the gospel into unreached fields need mission structures in partnership with local churches.[18] Movement pioneers form missionary bands that become catalysts for evangelism in unreached fields, leading to initial discipleship, church formation, and church strengthening. These bands work in partnership with new and existing local churches. Neither the churches nor the bands control the other.[19] Paul's purpose was to bring the churches into the maturity of knowing the mind of Christ and obedience to the gospel. They became interdependent partners with Paul and his missionary band.

5. Contagious Relationships

God exists in community as Father, Son, and Holy Spirit; the very nature of God is relationship. Made in his image, humanity reflects the relational character of God. Jesus understood the importance of relationships and shaped his mission around relational ties. He trained his disciples to go into unreached villages and look for responsive households that would become the entry point to the whole community. He led by example in his encounters with the Gerasene demoniac (Mark 5:1–18), Zacchaeus the tax-collector (Luke 19:1–9), and the Samaritan woman (John 4:1–26). Through these individuals, the good news about Jesus reached entire communities.

The key to the rapid growth of any movement is face-to-face recruitment within pre-existing social networks. The stronger the social network, the faster the movement spreads. But for a movement to grow, it must not only reach new people, it must keep them—and it must build them into a committed force for change. Movements made up of a collection of casual acquaintances will lack energy, commitment, and focus. A successful movement is a tight social network. However, if a movement is too tight, it will become isolated; it may keep its members, but it will not grow. In closed groups, internal relationships can be so strong that they exclude significant relationships with outsiders. This social isolation limits the ability to recruit. Growth can only continue if the movement remains both a tight and open social network. Jesus ministered to the crowds, but he didn't entrust himself to them unless they responded to his call to become disciples. He formed his disciples into a tight social network that maintained its openness to other people.

A multiplying movement is both tight and open. A tight but closed movement (fundamentalism) may retain its purity, but it won't reach outsiders. A movement that is open to society but has loose internal ties (liberalism) will become just like the world its members were once trying to save.

6. Rapid Mobilization

Movements don't spread if paid professionals are solely responsible for the work of missions. The movement Jesus started grew rapidly through the efforts of ordinary people equipped by missionaries such as the Twelve apostles, the apostle Paul, and his coworkers. That's why the Greek philosopher Celsus complained that the new faith was spread from house to house "by wool-workers, cobblers, laundry-workers, and the most illiterate and bucolic yokels" who claimed that they alone knew the right way to live.[20]

Jesus bypassed religious professionals and went looking for ordinary people. He commanded fishermen to follow him and promised to teach them to fish for people (Mark 1:17; Matthew 4:19). Some disciples followed him throughout Israel, but he sent others home to share what God had done for them (Mark 5:18–20). He taught them God's Word and promised them that the power of the Holy Spirit would enable them to make disciples of the nations (Acts 1:8). Christ gave the Great Commission to every disciple, not professionals. Every disciple is charged with making disciples by going, baptizing, and teaching those who respond to obey everything Jesus has commanded. Every disciple has the Word, the Spirit, and the responsibility to fulfill the Mission.

The New Testament names around one hundred people who were associated with Paul.[21] He refers to thirty-six of them with terms like "brother," "apostle," "fellow-worker," and "servant." He rarely traveled alone. He had nine key team members who worked with him, many of whom came from the churches he started. As he moved on to unreached cities, he expected the churches to partner with him in the Mission and to continue to reach their region in depth. He was confident he could move on as he committed the new churches to the Word and the Spirit (Acts 20:28, 32).

The church is a living organism that grows through its union with Christ. The church's missionary advance comes from the spontaneous, individual activity of its members led by the Holy Spirit. Institutional control produces sterility, whereas in a dynamic movement, the Word, the Spirit, and the Mission provide the necessary boundaries that shape its Identity. Controlled converts may not go astray, but they will produce nothing, whereas movement pioneers build the relational ties of support and accountability between practitioners.[22] In a declining movement, control comes from the center. Mass mobilization is replaced by professional clergy who pastor settled churches and teach in academic institutions.

7. Adaptive Methods

Adaptive Methods are one of the four elements of Strategy. They are the Methods that enable a movement to thrive within its changing environment and expand into new fields. Adaptive

Methods are simple, reproducible, sustainable, and scalable.

It's important to note that not all Methods are necessarily Adaptive Methods. In practice, Methods will vary with context and may fall short of being Adaptive Methods. Jesus' Methods were simple, yet powerful: he trained his followers to do what he did—enter an unreached community and form a base of operations; his teaching and his stories were memorized and passed on; he trained workers on the job; his movement required no central funding or control. Likewise, expanding movements have simple but powerful Methods to equip every believer. Adaptive Methods enable a movement to both flex with its changing environment and to expand into new fields through ordinary people. A movement's commitment to both core convictions and expansion provides the creative tension for learning, renewal, and growth. In contrast, dying institutions are willing to sacrifice their unique identity; they are conservative in setting goals and unable to face the reality of their poor performance.[23]

Movements that remain true to their Identity (Word, Spirit, Mission) will test the effectiveness of their Methods and make changes that align with their Identity. A later case study will show how John Wesley had one mission—to disciple a nation. In pursuit of that mission he was continually experimenting, adapting his Methods for spreading the gospel, making disciples, forming groups, and mobilizing workers.

Some movements can suffer from "the failure of success."[24] Convinced that what they are doing is right, they stop paying attention to the world around them. They stop learning and adapting. The informal Methods that brought the initial success become formalized with inflexible procedures and structures. Creativity and innovation jump ship or must walk the plank. The solution is not to adopt the latest fad in Methods, but to revisit how Methods can best serve Identity and Strategy.

CONCLUSION

Jesus is the pioneer and perfecter of our faith (Hebrews 12:2). His example is ours to follow. Like Jesus, we must obey the living Word of God, depend on the Holy Spirit, and fulfill the Mission he gave to us. These are the heart and soul of a multiplying movement as a work of God. Identity leads to effective patterns of ministry—Pioneering Leaders, Contagious Relationships, Rapid Mobilization, and Adaptive Methods—which are clearly evident in the mission of Jesus, the apostles, and the church.

Life and renewal come through the Word, the Spirit, and the Mission. Decline and decay inevitably follow when we drift from these essentials of Identity. (In chapter seven we'll look at how Identity is essential to the renewal and rebirth of declining movements.) As we examine each stage, we'll see how Identity is the key that determines the rise and fall of movements. We'll note Identity's impact on the four patterns of Strategy, as only when the Word, the Spirit, and the Mission are prioritized will it be possible to address these issues.

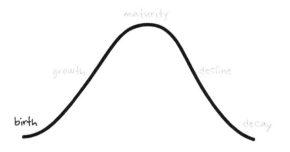

2. BIRTH
COMMIT TO THE CAUSE

He went out half-naked in his hair-shirt into the winter woods, walking the frozen ground between the frosty trees; a man without a father. He was penniless, he was parentless, he was to all appearance without a trade or a plan or a hope in the world; and as he went under the frosty trees, he burst suddenly into song.

—G.K. Chesterton

Francis' father was furious. He had endured his son's wild living, but Pietro Bernardone would not allow Francis to squander the family's wealth on the poor. He dragged Francis before the Bishop of Assisi for a ruling. As a rich silk merchant, Bernardone had plans for his son to one day take over the business and become a leading man in the city of Assisi, but Francis disappointed him.

In AD 1201, Francis left his home seeking adventure as a soldier. He fought with Assisi's forces against the city of Perugia and was captured, imprisoned, and later ransomed. On the way to his next battle, he heard a voice ask, "Is it better to obey the servant or the Lord?" When he answered, "Lord, what would you have me do?" he was told to return home and wait. As he waited, Francis became overwhelmed by the emptiness of his life. Looking for answers, Francis made a pilgrimage to Rome, and on the steps of St. Peter's Basilica, he exchanged clothes with a beggar and begged for his dinner.

After Francis returned to Assisi, he was praying in the broken-down church of St. Damian when a voice spoke to him from the cross: "Go and restore my house." Taking the command literally, he rode to his father's store and loaded his horse with fine fabrics. Selling the cloth and the horse, he used the money to minister to the needy and restore the church at St. Damian. Furious, his father brought him before the bishop for a ruling. The bishop sympathized with Francis' generosity but ruled the money was not his to give away. Francis responded by stripping naked and laying his clothes at his father's feet. He renounced his family ties and inheritance, declaring his trust in his heavenly Father to provide. Bernardone gathered up his son's clothes and left, while the bishop wrapped his cloak around a trembling Francis. So began the Franciscan movement.

HOW MOVEMENTS ARE BORN

Founders are dreamers. Whereas realists adapt themselves to the world, founders of movements want to change their world.[1] They don't know enough to know it can't be done. Before there was ever the Franciscan Order, there was Francis and those who followed him because they believed in the cause he embodied. Great founders such as Francis deal in meaning; they trade in what is important. They rally people around a great cause—one that is worth living and dying for, and inspires people to act. Although a movement may make use of methods and organizational forms, it is not an organization: it's a cause.

I've learned that Founders have five important tasks to complete, and Francis of Assisi excelled in each one:

1. Wrestle with God
2. Fuel discontent
3. Dare to dream
4. Commit to action
5. Build a team

1. Wrestle with God

Like the patriarch Jacob, great movement founders wrestle with God in the wilderness. As they surrender, their Identity is found, and calling flows from their encounter. A renewed awareness of God's authority frees a founder to question existing authorities and call God's people back to biblical realities and a new direction. In the struggle, founders learn obedience to the Word and Spirit, and faithfulness to God's call.

Rejected by his father, Francis begged for stones to restore ruined churches in the countryside around Assisi. In the chapel of Portiuncula, he read Jesus' instructions to his disciples:

> *"As you go, proclaim this message: 'The kingdom of heaven has come near.' Heal the sick, raise the dead, cleanse those who have leprosy, drive out demons. Freely you have received; freely give. Do not get any gold or silver or copper to take with you in your belts— no bag for the journey or extra shirt or sandals or a staff, for the worker is worth his keep."*
>
> MATTHEW 10:7–10

Through his struggle, Francis found God's calling: He would do what Jesus commanded and proclaim the message of the kingdom of heaven, trusting God to provide everything he needed.

Founders like Francis must embody the cause they champion because at this stage nothing exists apart from their commitment to the cause. That's why the story begins for Jesus in the wilderness where his Identity is tested and proved. Transformation is costly. The apostle Paul received his call while lying face down on the road to Damascus. For the next three days he sat blinded, not knowing what would come next, completely dependent on God to rescue him (Acts 9). All his strength turned to weakness, and this dependence on God became the heart of the multiplying movement he helped birth.

2. Fuel discontent

Founders are unreasonable people, refusing to accept the world as it is. Movements are born because something needs to change. Founders help people see what's wrong and how to put things right. Movement founders raise the levels of discontent by pointing to the gap between *what is* and *what should be.*

For 900 years, monasticism had been the dominant force for the renewal and spread of the Christian faith. In the early thirteenth century, monasticism was in crisis. The movement that began in the desert caves of Egypt as a protest against worldliness was itself corrupt and declining. Monasticism had thrived in the rural and feudal societies. However, as towns and cities grew throughout Europe a new form of religious order was required to reach the rapidly growing urban populations.[2] Under the leadership of Rome, the church became a burden on the common people. The poorest workers were compelled to pay tithes that enriched the absentee clergy, rivaled only by the nobility and wealthy merchants. Exchanging the mission of Jesus for wealth and security, the monastic orders had abandoned poverty to live in comfort. Francis of Assisi refused to accept the gap between the monastic ideal and everyday reality; eventually, thousands followed his example.

Founders draw urgent attention to what must be put right. They exploit the gap between how things are and how they should be. The ideal-real gap is the gap between ideals and reality.[3] Most people prefer the certainty and the known realm of reality—why seek uncertainty if we can live with what we have now? We compromise, learning to live with the gap between reality and the ideal. However, founders like Francis refuse to accept the ideal-real gap, and in doing so they make everyone else feel uncomfortable. Founders are impatient and uncompromising. They see the deficiencies and will not tolerate them. The old paradigm no longer fits reality and the need for change becomes urgent. The founder must highlight a problem that doesn't yet have proven solutions and in doing so raises more questions than answers. While the problems with the status quo are real, the solutions are not, and so the new paradigm must be accepted by faith.[4]

Founders heighten the ideal-real gap. They sell the problem. They inject urgency. They offer hope for a better future.

3. Dare to dream

Founders fuel discontent—but a critique without a dream results in paralysis and cynicism.

Francis' dream was to live life like Jesus and his disciples did—as an apostolic brotherhood with no distinction between clergy and laity, living in obedience to God's leading, and without the hindrance of possessions. The motivation for this was a passionate love for Christ. Bonaventure, a follower of Francis, described him as "completely absorbed by the fire of divine love like a glowing coal."[5] Francis' response to the decline of settled monasticism was the birth of mobile missionary bands of friars (brothers). Wherever they went, they preached the joy of repentance, and trusted God for their needs. Francis and many of his followers came from wealthy and noble families, but they made the poor and the outcast the special concern of the Order. This was part of Francis' commitment to reach people for Christ outside the walls of the cloister and the borders of Christendom.

Like Francis, founders are dreamers. They cast vision for a better future. They may not know how they'll get there, but they know where they are going. Founders point the way because they can see the destination. They live their lives backward. The reality of the vision draws them into the future despite the obstacles. Yet, where does vision come from?

When I was a young church planter, I had no idea what I was doing. There was no training available, no books to read. I had four audio cassettes on church planting. I listened to them again and again. I knew I needed a vision and some values, but I was troubled by this. How would I get a vision? I just wanted to survive long enough to start a viable church. When God was ready, he went to work on me. When I finally surrendered to the work of God in me, vision came as a calling from God rather than from a brainstorming exercise. I learned that vision is a by-product of knowing God, sharing his heart, and understanding his purposes revealed in Scripture. Vision is the fruit of a surrendered life. It's his mission, not ours. What was true for me as a young church planter is true for movement founders. Vision is a gift. We don't set the agenda.

When Jesus rose from the dead, he encountered a shattered band of disciples. They were returning to their old way of life. He brought them back together and restored them. Jesus took these disciples on a journey through the Old Testament and explained God's purposes. He showed them how the Messiah had to suffer. He told them that repentance for the forgiveness of sins will be preached to all nations and that they must wait for the promised Holy Spirit (Luke 24:45–49). Vision came to the disciples because God revealed it. Jesus opened their minds to understand God's purposes in the Scriptures, and the Holy Spirit enabled them to become partners in this great cause.

4. Commit to action

Ideas are only dangerous if they are turned into action. Discontent without vision leads to cynicism, but a dream without action is a fantasy. Founders dream, and then they enact those dreams.

From the moment of his call in the chapel of Portiuncula, Francis determined to act and live as a disciple of Jesus. He became an itinerant missionary, preaching repentance. He renounced property and went without a money bag. He trusted God and imitated Christ in poverty and in his love for those in need. Francis embodied the cause to which he called others.

His leadership style was intuitive, impulsive, and inspirational. At a crossroad on one missionary journey, he prayed, then told the brother accompanying him to twirl like a top to determine which way they should go. Then off they went.

Founders aren't interested in gradual improvement. They call for deep change, going outside the existing structures to bring it about, and conflict often ensues.[6] Jesus looked at the rich young ruler with love and told him, "One thing you lack [...] Go, sell everything you have and give to the poor, and you will have treasure in heaven. Then come, follow me" (Mark 10:21). He stood and watched the young man walk away sad. Jesus refused to be bound by the expectations of those around him. He committed to action. Nothing would stop Jesus from seeking lost sheep. Similarly, movement founders live undivided lives.

5. Build a team

A committed founder is not a movement. Founders must attract committed followers. Because the movement is still in its infancy, founders don't have salaries, benefits, or positions of power to offer their recruits. Instead, they offer the reward of a cause worth living and dying for. They have intrinsic authority, possessing what sociologists call *charisma*.

There's a difference between "being the leader" and "leading." "Being the leader" means you have a title and a position. "Leading" means people want to follow you—not because they have to, not because they are paid to, but because they want to.[7]

Each of the Gospels record how Jesus called his first

disciples. Jesus' authority stands out. The disciples left everything to follow this Galilean carpenter who had no formal authority. The accounts of his baptism and wilderness testing reveal the true source of his authority.

Francis of Assisi was true to his calling, and his life drew others who were willing to lay down their lives. The people of Assisi couldn't decide if Francis was a saint or a madman. A few chose to believe he was a saint. Bernard of Quintavalle was a wealthy and prominent man, yet he sold his possessions and gave away his fortune to the poor, joining Francis as a beggar. Next came Peter Catanii, a lawyer. Within a year, Francis had eleven followers. As the numbers grew, Francis organized his followers into small traveling bands who preached repentance. The Franciscans preached in the open air, on street corners, in the market places, and in open fields. Speaking in the ordinary language of the people, their vivid messages inspired and moved people to repentance and joy before God. Francis was never ordained as a priest. Similarly, those who followed his lead were ordinary, untrained men, resented by the clergy for their success.

Like Francis, founders inspire others to act. They win the trust of followers by putting their lives on the line for the cause. They demonstrate the unconventional tactics that will achieve a movement's purposes and they protect it from those who bring their own agendas.

Jesus attracted large crowds of people, and they were the object of his love and his mission. But he never confused the people of the crowds with his disciples. The crowds were the lost sheep of the house of Israel (Matthew 10:6); the disciples were called out of those crowds and Jesus entrusted himself to them. Jesus' first disciples formed the nucleus of a missionary movement that took the good news to the world, sent out among the crowds to preach and to heal.

These are the five key tasks of Birth—wrestle with God, fuel discontent, dare to dream, commit to action, build a team. These five tasks are evidenced in the lives of all founders, such as Patrick of Ireland, William Carey, and John Wesley.[8]

FROM BIRTH TO GROWTH

There's no guarantee a movement will survive Birth and move into Growth. Infant mortality is a real possibility. The founder has to attract and mobilize the first band of committed followers. There are no salaries. No prestigious titles. No impressive facilities. There is a dream, the founder's commitment, and a call to action.

Francis of Assisi lived to see the Franciscan movement grow beyond all expectations. Friars were sent throughout Italy and to Germany, France, Greece, Spain, Portugal, Morocco, and Tunisia. They didn't know local languages and they were mistaken as heretics, yet their zeal kept them going. However, the movement was bittersweet. In his lifetime, Francis refused to accept the need for tighter organization. He hoped to follow Christ in simplicity and to inspire others to do likewise. The written Rule he composed to guide the movement contained principles, but how they were to be implemented was unclear. This gave the Franciscans flexibility, but it also caused harsh divisions.

In 1219, Francis set off with twelve companions for the Holy Land on a mission to Muslims. He hoped to win the Sultan of Egypt to faith in Christ and put an end to the Crusades—or die in the attempt. During his mission, Francis received an urgent message to return: the Franciscan Order was in crisis, becoming a divided movement. Some friars, craving permanency, had built a monastery. He ordered them to get rid of it. Others feared that what had begun as a people's movement was becoming an order of priests. Still other friars preferred a structured organization to the spontaneity of Francis' leadership.

After his mission to Muslims, Francis' effective leadership of the Order ceased. He spent the rest of his life alone and in prayer in a hermitage on Mount Alverno. In 1226, Francis died at Portiuncula, where he had received his missionary call. That year, the Franciscans founded new orders in Spain, France, and Portugal. The movement continued to grow and expand into England, Scotland, Austria, Hungary, Ireland, Denmark, Bohemia, Sweden, and Norway. By 1280, there were 20,000 members. By the end of that century they were at the farthest points of the known world. In 1350, there were 35,000 members.[9]

The expansion came with bitter conflict between Francis' strict followers, known as the Spirituals, and the moderates, who were called Conventuals. The church hierarchy backed the Conventuals. The Spirituals left to become a separate order.

The paradox of the Franciscan Order is that it experienced more internal conflict than any other order, yet it grew and expanded like no other. Dynamic movements that care about their core Identity will experience conflict. Such conflict can be productive when it is channeled into furthering the movement's cause. Diversity in methods around a common cause leads to innovation. As we'll see in the Quaker case study (chapter four), conflict between progressives and traditionalists becomes counterproductive when the goal is institutional survival rather than the cause for which the movement exists.

Francis of Assisi excelled as a founder and lived what he believed. His authority flowed from his uncompromising commitment to Christ. He had little time for organizational structures and external requirements. He excelled as a visionary but struggled to ensure the movement adapted to its meteoric rise. Regardless, he remains one of the most endearing figures of Christian history.

LEADERSHIP TASKS: BIRTH

- **Wrestle with God:** Surrender to God to bring clarity of vision.
- **Fuel discontent:** Raise awareness of the gap between the ideal and reality.
- **Dare to dream:** Know where you are going, even if you don't yet know how you'll get there.

- **Commit to action:** Show how the vision can be turned into reality.
- **Build a team:** Call people who are willing to lay down their lives for the cause.

CONCLUSION

There is nothing more powerful than an idea whose time has come. But ideas don't make history—committed people do. A movement is born when someone commits to action—and others follow them.

The greatest danger during Birth is the possibility that the founder loses heart. Founders must commit to the cause because they believe it is right, not because it "works." They must surrender to God, obey his Word, depend in weakness upon his Holy Spirit, and devote themselves to the Mission— even when there is no evidence of success. This is what Jesus did in the wilderness, in the garden, and on the cross. He entrusted himself to the One who raises the dead.

Movements that make it through Birth must face the challenge of Growth, turning the idea into effective Strategies and Methods that get results.

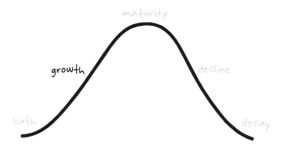

3. GROWTH
PUT THE IDEA TO WORK

John Wesley sought no less than the recovery of the truth, life, and power of earliest Christianity and the expansion of that kind of Christianity.

—George Hunter III

No one would have predicted that John Wesley would be among the great founders and builders of a multiplying movement. Wesley, the founder of Methodism, went to America hoping to convert the Indians. But he returned to England despairing of his own salvation, wondering, "Who shall convert me?"[1]

On May 24, 1738, Wesley reluctantly attended a study on the book of Romans. As the leader was describing the change that God works in the heart through faith in Christ, Wesley felt his heart "strangely warmed." He wrote in his journal, "I felt I did trust in Christ alone for salvation; and an assurance was given me that He had taken away my sins, even mine, and saved me from the law of sin and death."[2]

Transformed by God's grace, Wesley traveled Britain with a vision for the conversion and discipling of a nation and the renewal of a fallen church. His passion drew others to the cause. Wesley initiated the Birth of the Methodist movement and led it into Growth. Wesley showed how a movement leader in Growth turns vision into action while maintaining flexibility and control. He released authority and responsibility, and empowered the movement to embody the Methodist cause. A movement that completes the following four tasks is set up to focus on a fifth—pursuing Prime. In Prime a movement knows why it exists, where it's going, and how to get there.[3]

These are the tasks in Growth:

1. Put the idea to work
2. Balance flexibility and control
3. Release authority and responsibility
4. Let go
5. Pursue Prime

1. Put the idea to work

Growth is not the time for generating more ideas. It's the time to put ideas to work. Visionaries must become doers who turn dreams into reality by inspiring others to follow their example.

In March of 1739, Wesley knew it was time to act. He headed to Bristol, invited by the evangelist George Whitefield. Wesley was shocked by what he saw; he believed Whitefield was acting like an extremist and heretic by preaching in the open air to vast crowds. On a Sunday afternoon, Wesley watched Whitefield preach to 30,000 people. The fruit of Whitefield's methods changed his mind. The next day Wesley preached outdoors. By September, he was preaching to crowds of 12,000–20,000.

The common people were less likely to attend church, so Wesley went to them, and he was gladly received. He preached to thousands, standing on a tombstone with the church behind him serving as a sounding board. He preached in market squares. He preached in public parks in the evenings and on the weekends. He preached at 5:00 a.m. before the workday began. Wesley adopted methods from other movements and shaped them to his purpose. Whitefield showed him how to reach the masses through open air preaching. The Moravians taught him how to gather them into disciple making groups.

In the early stages of Growth, founders are carried forward by conviction and intuition, not evidence. Like David standing before Goliath, they don't have all the answers but are willing to take a risk. They are willing to do something. They draw action-orientated people who likewise are motivated by conviction, not proof. Once there is action and progress, others will come on board, and the movement picks up momentum.

2. Balance flexibility and control

In the early stages of Growth, it's too soon for the founder to release authority. The Identity of the movement is still forming, but decisions must be made regarding Strategy and Methods. If the leader steps back now, competing agendas will undermine a movement's Identity. The founder must lead by example and keep everyone focused on getting the results for which the movement exists.

Movements don't live by passion alone. A movement must develop Strategies and Methods if it is to spread beyond the founding group. There's a dilemma: systems reduce flexibility—yet flexibility without systems and structure results in chaos and fragmentation, as the Franciscans experienced. In Growth, the movement must remain flexible if it is to adapt to its environment. A dynamic movement is like a gymnast balancing flexibility and control, stability and change.[4] Wesley did this to great effect. In the 1740s he explored and adapted Strategies and Methods that served a growing movement. These included field preaching, classes, bands, societies, itinerants, circuits, annual conferences, and publications. He borrowed from other movements, constantly implementing, adapting, and evaluating. He combined the elements into a consistent whole that became Methodism.

Wesley's flexibility with Strategy and Methods was

tempered by his dependence on the authority of the Word, the leading of the Holy Spirit and his clarity of Mission. He loved church tradition, but for Wesley, the Bible was "the only standard of truth, and the only model of pure religion." He said, "I allow no other rule, whether of faith or practice, than the Holy Scriptures."[5] This view of Scripture left him free to experiment by dispensing with church traditions that no longer served a purpose. He adapted his methods under the guidance of the Holy Spirit as he pursued the Mission of discipling a nation. Wesley experimented, tested, and refined simple but effective methods and structures, so the movement could expand but still remain focused once it moved beyond his direct control. His Spirit-inspired Adaptive Methods enabled him to mobilize leaders and workers in an expanding movement and still keep it on track. Methodist Identity remained clear. Wesley's Methods were Adaptive Methods—simple, scalable, and reproducible. These simple patterns and structures enabled the movement to grow in depth and breadth (flexibility) while remaining true to its Identity (control).

Two sets of Adaptive Methods allowed for depth (societies, classes, and bands) and breadth (circuits and circuit riders) in an expanding movement:

A. Societies, classes, and bands

Wesley was now preaching to crowds of thousands. But his mission didn't stop with people who made decisions—he wanted disciples. He could have become the pastor-teacher of a great church, but he wanted to reach a nation. He needed a simple method for discipleship in a rapidly expanding movement.[6] So wherever the gospel was met with faith, he set up Methodist societies. He formed the first of these in London in an unused cannon foundry.

Methodist societies were the functional equivalent of a local church. Society meetings included worship, Bible reading, a message, and prayer. The use of the term "society" enabled Wesley to avoid conflict with the state-sponsored Anglican church as he reinvented the nature of church. After Wesley's death, Methodist societies became Methodist churches. Wesley divided each society into classes, which were groups of twelve with an appointed leader. The condition for membership was a desire to flee from the wrath and to come and show the reality of conversion through conduct.[7] As class leaders visited members they discovered behavior incompatible with true conversion, such as domestic disputes and drunkenness.[8] In response, Wesley turned the class meeting into a pastoral and disciplinary structure, which became the building block of a disciple making movement.[9]

The purpose of field preaching was to gather those seeking salvation into the societies and classes. Most conversions took place in the classes, and those converted then joined bands, which were even smaller discipleship groups. The focus of the class was conversion and discipline. The focus of the band was the confession of sin and pastoral care. Through the system of societies, classes, and bands, Methodists came together to encourage each other, confess their sins, pray for each other, and hold one another accountable. The class leaders were the backbone of the movement. Wesley examined them to determine "their grace, their gifts, and their manner of meeting their several classes."[10] Discipline and accountability were Wesley's effective methods for dealing with an expanding movement.[11]

Overwhelmed with opportunities, Wesley experimented with evangelistic preaching that wasn't followed up with new societies, classes, and bands. It was a failure. Wesley observed, "Almost all the seed has fallen by the wayside; there is scarce any fruit of it remaining." The awakened souls could not "watch over one another in love," and believers could not "build up one another and bear one another's burdens."[12]

Balancing flexibility and control enabled Wesley to build a movement of committed followers who shared the call to disciple a nation.

B. Circuits and circuit riders

Wesley could not disciple a nation alone. He multiplied himself through a system of circuits and circuit riders.

London and Bristol—the cities under Wesley's direct influence—were the movement's strongholds. Methodism was also springing up across the nation because of local revivals. It further expanded by adopting local groups and leaders from outside the movement. Inevitably, this added both momentum and new challenges, as the absorbed groups came with many theologies and practices—Calvinists, Moravians, Baptists, and Quakers.[13] How would Wesley unite pockets of revival into a cohesive movement? Leadership was key. He and his brother Charles were constantly on the road both advancing and unifying the movement. In an expanding movement the founder must not depend on positional authority but on the authority of a life devoted to the Word, the Spirit, and the Mission.

By 1746, Wesley had societies in seven circuits: London, Bristol, Cornwall, Evesham, Yorkshire, Newcastle, and Wales. The strategy was for two or three field preachers to saturate a region with evangelistic preaching and organize societies, classes, and bands. They would identify local leaders before moving on to the unreached region. The preachers multiplied Wesley's ability to both expand and consolidate Methodism. Within two years there were thirty-six circuit riders in nine circuits across Britain. These circuit riders were the Pioneering Leaders responsible for evangelism in unreached fields and the formation of the societies, classes, and bands.

By balancing flexibility and control, Wesley formed Methodism into a movement with the effective strategies and Adaptive Methods required to pursue its mission. He was attending to the chief task of a founder in Growth—building a movement that would outlast him.

3. Release authority and responsibility

In Birth, the founder must draw together the first group of committed followers. They follow the founder's direct example.

To move from Birth to Growth, founders must mobilize leaders who multiply their impact. Wesley made sure these movement pioneers carried the Identity of the Methodist movement with them. Wesley trained leaders who were biblically sound, spiritually alive, and effective in pioneering ministry. Every year Wesley examined his preachers at an annual conference and would dismiss them if they were unsuitable. Most circuit riders lacked formal education, so Wesley trained them on the job through a stream of publications.[14] Wesley also used the annual conference to include his preachers in the shaping of the movement.[15] Together they clarified doctrine, adapted their methods and structures, and planned for growth.

Wesley was a great evangelist and pioneer, but that didn't make him a movement leader. He was a movement leader because his focus was not on himself but on developing others who owned the Methodist cause. In doing this, the movement expanded well beyond his immediate influence.

By 1750, the building blocks of the Methodist movement were in place:

- Societies, bands, and classes at a local level, connected nationally
- Monthly "Watch Night" services for prayer
- "Love Feasts" every few months where society members met to share a simple meal and their stories of God's activity

- Regions divided into circuits opened up by traveling preachers
- An annual conference for circuit riders that settled doctrinal issues and checked the health and advancement of the movement

Great leaders give their people freedom and responsibility within a framework. Wesley shaped a culture, refined Methodism's Adaptive Methods, and gave ordinary people authority and responsibility. Methodism became a disciplined movement of pioneers, supported by local leaders.

A leader's greatest legacy is the cause they leave behind and the people aligned with that cause. Multiplication can take place when the founder releases authority and responsibility to people who know why the movement exists (Identity), how to pursue its mission (Strategy), and what to do (Methods).

4. Let go

In the early stages, the founder's commitment sustains a movement. Yet if that loving embrace lasts too long, it will end in suffocation. The movement will be caught in the Founder's Trap.[16] The Founder's Trap occurs when a founder remains in direct personal control and won't release authority and responsibility. Similar to the motion of a yo-yo, the founder releases control, then snatches it back again. The founder lets go, grabs control back again, lets it go, grabs it back …[17] If the founder remains in control, the movement will stall. Founders overcome this challenge by focusing on the movement, not on themselves. They must develop action-oriented leaders who embrace the cause; they need to build a culture of discipline around Identity; and they need Strategies and Methods that align the movement with Identity. In these later stages of Growth, founders must learn to lead without being in control. Interestingly, Methodism's greatest expansion came in the generation *after* Wesley's death. The drive came from leaders who knew Wesley's example, his writings, and his methods.[18]

Growth begins with the founder in control: the founder must embody the heart of the movement, and the founder must keep everyone and everything aligned with the cause. But the founder is not the movement. Caught in the Founder's Trap, a movement cannot grow beyond the direct control of its founder; a controlling founder will continue to rule by personal decree and tight structures that don't allow for initiative. Emerging leaders will leave in frustration or be forced out.

The best antidote for the Founder's Trap is a mission that extends beyond the limitations of one individual. Wesley's vision extended across his nation and soon reached around the world. His followers were inspired by his example, despite having never met him. But there was something more at work. Wesley learned from Jesus' example as a founder. When Jesus left this earth, his disciples had the memory of his life and teaching. But they had more than a memory: Jesus led them into the same relationship he had with the Father and the Holy Spirit. He told them it was for their good that he went away

(John 16:7). His physical absence enhanced their leadership. Through the Word and the Spirit, his presence went with every disciple as they pursued the Mission he gave them. Wesley brought others into the same experience of saving grace he encountered. He mobilized them into an army of committed followers who embraced the Methodist cause. They knew who they were, and they knew what to do. The movement had vitality and form, enabling it to surpass the direct control of its founder.

5. Pursue Prime

Growth begins with the challenge of putting the idea to work. Once the idea is working, the movement is making tangible progress: it is attracting Pioneering Leaders and expanding its impact; it has both control and flexibility; its clear Strategy and Adaptive Methods empower followers to achieve the movement's purpose; the movement embodies the founding ideal and is no longer dependent upon its founder. Now it has a chance of reaching what Ichak Adizes calls *Prime*.

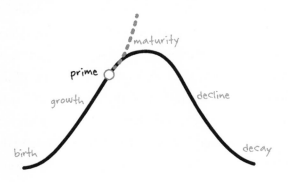

In Prime an organization knows why it exists, where it is going, and how to get there.[19] It is achieving the results for which it was created. Organizations in Prime confront the brutal facts when they fall short, and adjust accordingly. The organization remains creative and flexible, ensuring long-term effectiveness.

Methodism experienced Prime when it crossed the Atlantic Ocean and came under the leadership of Francis Asbury. When the American War of Independence broke out in 1776, all but two Methodist ministers returned to England. They left behind 600 members and a young English missionary named Francis Asbury. Methodism not only survived the Revolutionary War—it swept the land. When Asbury died in 1816, there were 200,000 Methodists. By 1850, there were one million Methodists led by 4,000 itinerants and 8,000 local preachers. The only organization more extensive was the U.S. government.[20]

Although he never spent extended time with his hero, Asbury was a disciple of John Wesley. He put aside all other books except the Bible and Wesley's writings. Asbury refined the movement's Adaptive Methods to fit the American context while ensuring Methodism remained true to its original spirit.[21] The Methodist system of circuit riders was ideally suited to handle the rapid geographic expansion of the early Republic.[22] Class meetings remained the building blocks of the movement. Freed of the constraints of state-sponsored religion, North American Methodism embraced its identity as a church planting movement. Methodism under Asbury outstripped the strongest and most established denominations in the new nation. In 1775, Methodists accounted for only 2.5 percent of total church membership in America. By 1850, their share had risen to 34 percent, and this was when Methodist requirements for membership were far stricter than those of other denominations. For every Methodist member, there were at least ten adherents. In 1805, Asbury estimated a membership of 100,000, with one million regular attenders.[23]

Prime is a moving target, not a destination. Yesterday's Adaptive Methods become today's rules and regulations. To maintain Prime, a movement must continually confront reality and return to its Identity—commitment to the Word, the Spirit, and the Mission. It must also rediscover and apply effective Strategies—Pioneering Leaders, Contagious Relationships, Rapid Mobilization, and Adaptive Methods.

LEADERSHIP TASKS: GROWTH

- **Put the idea to work:** Ground the founding vision in effective action that produces the results for which the movement exists.
- **Balance flexibility and control:** Utilize effective methods and functional structures that enable the spread of the movement.
- **Release authority and responsibility:** Mobilize workers and leaders to consolidate and expand the movement.

- **Let go:** Avoid the Founder's Trap by empowering the movement to embody the cause.
- **Pursue Prime:** Put in place the people and systems to achieve the results for which the movement exists.

CONCLUSION

Eventually Methodism drifted into Maturity, Decline, and Decay. But along the way it became the unplanned parent and grandparent of other dynamic movements—the Primitive Methodists, the Wesleyans, the Nazarenes, the Free Methodists, the Holiness movement, the Salvation Army, and Pentecostalism.

There is no guarantee that a movement will reach Prime or, having reached it, will remain there. Approaching the peak of the movement lifecycle, a movement must overcome the complacency that comes with success. Will it continue to renew itself or play it safe and protect its hard-earned gains? Maturity comes when a movement chooses security over Identity.

4. MATURITY
ENJOYING THE VIEW

I fear, wherever riches have increased ... the essence of religion, the mind that was in Christ, has decreased in the same proportion. Therefore do I not see how it is possible ... for any revival of true religion to continue long. For religion must necessarily produce both industry and frugality; and these cannot but produce riches. But as riches increase, so will pride, anger, and love of the world in all its branches.

—John Wesley

A movement in Maturity has plateaued, reaching the pinnacle of its success and is content. Life is good. The movement is still achieving significant results. But there is a loss of urgency and with that loss, creativity and adaptability are diminished.

The attitude is, "Why should we change? Let's keep doing what brought us success." Formality, order, and predictability matter more than getting results.[1] At its best, a movement risks everything to achieve its purpose—that's how movements remain young and vital. Movements mature when they choose to enjoy and protect their achievements. Momentum carries the movement forward but at a declining rate.

It took three hundred years, but, under the protection of the Emperor Constantine, the movement Jesus founded made its peace with the world and settled down. Movements tire of maintaining the tension with the world around them. They begin on the fringe of society but eventually want a seat at the table of acceptance. Movements can be blinded by their own success, as the story of the Quakers will show.

GEORGE FOX AND THE QUAKERS

In 1650, George Fox stood before a judge in Derby, England, charged with blasphemy, and facing six months in jail.[2] As Justice Bennet considered the sentence, the young man urged him to tremble in fear of God. The judge had heard that in their meetings Fox and his followers shook and trembled with emotion. He told Fox, "You folk are the tremblers, you are the quakers." The name *Quaker* stuck.[3]

Longing to experience God, Fox left home at nineteen. He lived rough, sleeping in barns and under bridges. He fasted and prayed. He sought answers from priests and pastors but found none. When he had lost hope, he heard a voice saying,

"There is one, even Christ Jesus, that can speak to thy condition."[4] Fox experienced the reality he sought—direct and unmediated access to God—bypassing priests and rituals. The Quaker movement was born.

The time was ripe for the Quakers' message. The English Civil War had left people disillusioned with both the established church and the Puritans. Thousands across the north of England were eager to encounter God. Fox wrote how at a meeting in Carlisle "the dreadful power of the Lord" was among them; people shook and trembled—even the building shook, and they feared it might fall down.[5] Quakers objected to priests whose wealthy lifestyles were paid for by the compulsory tithes of the poor. They denounced the aristocracy and gentry, lawyers and priests, the rich and powerful. As the movement grew, the secular and church authorities became alarmed and began to arrest them. By 1660, over 4,000 Quakers were imprisoned in appalling conditions. Hundreds died in custody. Mobs attacked Quakers as they worshipped and destroyed their meeting houses.[6] The first Quaker preachers to arrive in Cambridge were whipped in the marketplace until their flesh was torn. It made no difference to the authorities that these preachers were women.[7]

Quaker trials became opportunities for Quakers to preach and evangelize. Persecution only strengthened their resolve, but then the tide turned. In 1689, the Act of Toleration marked the end of official persecution. When George Fox died in 1691, he left behind a thriving religious movement that had weathered the storm and emerged as a national organization that was expanding into Europe and North America.

Rejected by society, Quakers had forged deep ties with each other. Once the persecution stopped, those ties were utilized for individual and corporate success. The Quakers prospered, but acceptance proved to be more dangerous to their movement than persecution.

There are three key factors that contribute to the plateauing of movements:

1. Stumbling over success
2. Ignoring the ideal-real gap
3. Choosing extremes

1. Stumbling over success

A movement that has succeeded in the Growth phase is prone to arrogance. Hard lessons are forgotten. Progress is taken for granted. Movements settle down and enjoy their achievements.

In the late 1690s, a Welsh Quaker family moved to Birmingham, England, to escape persecution. They did well in iron production and lent money to local manufacturers. Their business became Lloyds Bank, which today is the largest retail bank in Britain. They weren't the only Quakers who prospered. Between 1700–1750, Quakers controlled over half of the iron industry in England and Wales.[8] The British cocoa and chocolate industry owes its origin almost entirely to Quakers. In 1824, John Cadbury, a Quaker from Birmingham, sold tea, coffee, and drinking chocolate. By 1854, Cadbury was supplying chocolate to Queen Victoria.[9]

Why were the formerly outcast Quakers so successful? Quakers held themselves to the highest standards of personal and business ethics. Consumers, lenders, suppliers, and workers in the surrounding society all wanted to deal with Quakers because they could be trusted. Their lifestyle was austere, they were committed to honesty, hard work, and simplicity. They withdrew from the frivolity of society, but their faith led them to be actively involved in the world through their work as an expression of God's will. Both the personal and commercial activities of individual Quakers were examined in their local meetings, with an expectation that every Quaker would live up to Quaker standards.[10] Quakers excelled in the fields of education, industry, science, and commerce. Quaker companies provided housing, schooling, and welfare for their employees. Elizabeth Fry, a prominent Quaker, led the nation in prison reform, and Quakers were major players in the abolition of slavery in Britain and the United States.

Toward the end of his life, George Fox saw how their faith had made the Quakers rich and influential—but in prosperity they had lost their zeal to spread that faith at home and abroad. Just days before his death in 1691, Fox condemned those Quakers "who embrace the present world and encumber themselves with their own businesses and neglect the Lord's and so are good for nothing."[11]

The movement was divided. Progressives wanted to engage

with the world through commercial activities and social reform. Traditionalists wanted to withdraw and preserve the integrity of the Quakers. Conflict between the two groups sapped the movement's vitality, and the number of Quakers declined from 66,000 in 1680 to less than 14,000 in 1861.[12] The Quakers stumbled when they were at the peak of their power and influence, experiencing just one generation of exponential growth.

The failure of success is as old as the people of God. When God redeemed Israel out of slavery, he led them into the wilderness where he prepared them to live in the promised land, by teaching them to obey his commands. Before they crossed the Jordan River, the Lord told them they were coming into a good land where they would prosper, but in their success, they must be careful not to become proud and forget the Lord. Israel was instructed to remember and obey him and not pursue other gods—or they would be destroyed. In their success they failed to remember (Deuteronomy 8).

As Wesley observed, faith brings hard work, honesty, and discipline. With God's blessing, prosperity ensues and the benefits overflow into society. These things are good, yet success also breeds arrogance and the love of this world, and the hearts of God's people can grow cold.

2. Ignoring the ideal-real gap

Movements emerge because something needs to change—something must be put right. New movements fuel discontent, but it's hard to maintain the tension. Successful movements become content; they want to relieve the tension with the world in which they live.

The Quakers' faith had catapulted them into a new world, yet it also placed them at odds with it. As their businesses thrived, they were increasingly aware they were out of step with culture. They wanted to fit in and wanted to cling to what they had gained. They wanted their faith to be less demanding and more acceptable.

Movements stay young by maintaining the creative tension between what is (reality) and what should be (ideal). Movements grow old when they ignore the ideal-real gap, when they protect their accomplishments rather than risk adding to them.[13] In the battle between the real and the ideal, reality wins. Peter Senge explains it this way: imagine an elastic band stretched between your hands. One hand represents a better future, the other today's reality. Pull your hands apart, and the tension grows. The greater the distance, the greater the tension. Will you hold on to the ideal and cause reality to move toward it? Or will the vision be dragged down toward reality?[14]

Time is not the only factor in the aging of a movement. To stay youthful a movement must embrace the tension of the ideal-real gap.

3. Choosing extremes

In Maturity, a split can open up between traditionalists and progressives. Progressives want to reduce the tension of the ideal-real gap by reducing the demands on members and making the movement more socially acceptable. Traditionalists want to impose the stringency of the past, but without returning to the movement's original vitality. Progressives want the movement to be a loose social network open to society. Traditionalists want a tight social network closed to society. Both approaches fail because they are bereft of the inner reality that birthed the movement: they are adrift from their Identity.

The Quakers were caught between these two rival agendas: progressives wanted to lower the tension with society to suit their rising status in the world; traditionalists sought rigid adherence to traditional Quaker ways that would shut out the world. Traditionalists made sure those who "married out" of the movement were expelled. Between 1800 and 1855, almost half of all Quakers who married outside the movement either voluntarily left or were expelled. Many of those joined the rising tide of evangelicalism. The movement was paralyzed by conflict and loss of people.

Identity is the key to breaking the deadlock between traditionalists and progressives. A return to the essentials of Word, Spirit, and Mission would have meant a transition to a high-tension faith, connected with the surrounding culture, and making disciples throughout the world. Instead, the Quakers were caught between worldly success and backward-looking traditionalism. While the progressives and traditionalists battled it out, other evangelical movements benefited from the exodus of Quaker members.

The genius of George Fox was his emphasis on the individual's direct encounter with God through the Holy Spirit. Yet an inherent weakness of Quakerism was its over-reliance on this direct experience of the Holy Spirit at the expense of the Word. The Quakers lacked an emphasis on the written Word of God as a corrective to individualistic spirituality. They also lacked dedication to the clear mission to make disciples of the nations. Their energy for mission was poured into commercial success and transforming society. Meanwhile, their lack of urgency in multiplying disciples meant they ultimately lost their cultural influence.

THE ROAD BACK TO GROWTH

The Quakers did not return to the Growth phase; they drifted from Maturity to Decline. However, we do have a case study of a movement that stalled for a time and then continued its dramatic growth. It's found in the book of Acts.

Luke is the only Gospel writer who also wrote about the continuing story of the early church. He wrote his Gospel and the book of Acts as one story in two parts. Luke's Gospel tells the story of what Jesus began to do and teach (Acts 1:1). Acts is the account of what the risen Lord continued to do through his disciples, in the power of the Spirit. Luke wrote to challenge a new generation to continue the story and to remind the church of what it means to be a missionary movement.

Luke did not have unlimited space to record the events, so it should get our attention when he tells the story of Peter's encounter with Cornelius *three* times. It's the story of how the movement was in danger of settling down and missing the opportunity to reach the Gentile world. Maturing and declining movements hide from reality—they idealize the past but won't confront the present in the light of their mission. Sometimes it takes a dose of God's discipline to wake up a plateaued movement.

We pick up the narrative with Peter resting on the flat rooftop of Simon the Tanner's house in the coastal city of Joppa (Acts 10:9 ff.). As the story unfolds we'll see that these are the tasks required for a return to Growth:

1. Confront reality
2. Seize the opportunity
3. Remember who you are
4. Raise descendants

1. Confront reality

As Peter sat on the rooftop, he may have reflected on the progress of his assignment. He'd left Jerusalem and was on mission, strengthening the churches and seeing many more believe (Acts 9:32–43). As he traveled he was going deeper and deeper into Gentile territory. The Christian movement had spread like wildfire throughout Jerusalem and the surrounding villages. The churches were growing, not just in Jerusalem, but in Judea and north into Galilee; even the Samaritans had turned to Christ in large numbers (Acts 9:31). Amazingly, a God-fearing Ethiopian had repented, believed, and been baptized; we can imagine him returning home, telling the story of what God had done. Just as Jesus predicted, his followers had become witnesses in Jerusalem, Judea, Samaria, and to the ends of the earth (Acts 1:8).

But it had been ten years since Jesus had commanded his followers to make disciples of the nations—and no plans had been made for how this would be achieved. There was a general agreement that the gospel should go to the Gentiles, but no clarity about how non-Jews were to be added to the church. The early Christian movement was in danger of remaining a Jewish sect and missing its true purpose of making disciples of the nations. This was a movement near the peak of its early success, but in danger of missing the purpose of its very existence.

Peter needed to be confronted by the ideal-real gap. There was no urgency regarding the Gentile mission. Before there could be a solution, Peter needed to know there was a problem. God was about to restore the urgency of the mission and propel Peter into action. So as Peter nodded off to sleep, God intervened. He sent Peter a disturbing vision (Acts 10:9–16). The vision challenged Peter not to call anything unclean if God has declared it clean. Meanwhile, forty miles north along the coast in Caesarea, an angel had appeared to a Roman centurion named Cornelius (Acts 10:1–8). In response, Cornelius sent messengers to Peter, who by now was trying to make sense of his vision. The Spirit told Peter to go with these men without balking. Peter was clueless until God intervened. And even after God stepped in, Peter was slow to understand what was going on. This was the apostle Peter—trained by Jesus, filled with the Holy Spirit, leader of the Twelve. But this renewal of the Christian movement began with God, not Peter. It was not Peter's initiative. He must make his response, but God was in charge of the mission.

2. Seize the opportunity

When Peter arrived at Cornelius's house, it was full of Gentiles (Acts 10:24). While Cornelius was a God-fearer, probably some of his gathered friends were pagans. Peter hesitated before stepping inside because these Gentiles were unclean. But who was he to resist God?

As Peter preached the Word, the Spirit came in power, and these Gentile God-fearers and pagans turned and believed (Acts 10:44). Peter directed the Jewish believers who came with him to baptize the new converts. They were amazed that the Gentiles had received the Holy Spirit just as the Jewish disciples had at Pentecost (Acts 10:45–46). At Pentecost, Peter had announced that everyone who calls on the name of the Lord would be saved (Acts 2:21). Peter now understood the implications of his own preaching. This breakthrough was not instigated by Peter, or the Twelve, or the church in Jerusalem; God himself was responsible for the conversion of Cornelius and his household.

Although many Gentiles in Palestine could have been the focus of missionary outreach, no deliberate attempt had yet been made to reach them. At Pentecost the Holy Spirit was poured out on the first Jewish believers (Acts 2). The Samaritans had also received the Holy Spirit with power (Acts 8). Now the Gentiles had received the same Holy Spirit (Acts 10). God was gathering his people from all the nations of the world.

Peter departed a few days later, leaving behind a new community of disciples meeting in the home of Cornelius. Now he had a problem. How would he explain his actions to the Jewish believers in Jerusalem? The first Christians were Jews, and Jews didn't enter the house of uncircumcised Gentiles or eat their food. God had now shown Peter that Gentile believers were fully accepted without having to become Jews.

Peter had obeyed God's leading through that rooftop vision. He didn't play it safe and wait until after he had returned to Jerusalem to get agreement from the apostles, the elders, and the church. He acted immediately. God confirmed Peter's action when the Holy Spirit came upon the Gentiles as they heard the word of the gospel. What he did was consistent with the Word (as he now understood it), with the leading of the Spirit, and the Missionary task the risen Lord had entrusted to his disciples. He took a bold step of obedience on a strong foundation, knowing he would have to defend his decision.

God is the author of the renewal of the church in its Mission. We must follow Peter's example of obedience to the Word and the Spirit—even if the immediate result is confusion and conflict.

3. Remember who you are

The renewal of a movement must include God's call to remember. Throughout the Scriptures, God calls his people to remember his acts in their history.[15] They are to remember those events and their meaning. God's acts reveal the truth, the character, and the nature of God. They show his will for his people.[16] Remembering is more than recalling certain events and truths about God; it means a return to faith and obedience. The purpose is to retrieve the past and make it serve the present. There's no renewal until a movement remembers. Movements are renewed when they make a fresh return to Identity; a movement must return to where it began, reminding itself of its Identity as it moves forward in a fresh way.[17]

Peter successfully showed how the Gentile mission was God's intention, revealed in Scripture. He helped prepare the way for Paul and others to pursue that mission. When Peter returned to Jerusalem, traditionalists insisted that Gentile believers must be circumcised and that they must obey the Mosaic law. At the Council of Jerusalem, the debate raged, and Peter had to defend his actions. The fruit of God's intervention in the life and mission of the early church was conflict; important matters that went to the heart of the gospel were at stake. When a movement stumbles over success and enters Maturity, things must get worse before they'll get better.

On what basis does the Council of Jerusalem come to one mind on this important matter? How did God lead them? God changed Peter's heart; he brought him to repentance. Through Peter's strong but humble leadership, God brought his people back to their Identity—Word, Spirit, and Mission. When Peter spoke, he gave an honest account of his own lack of initiative in the Gentile mission and his initial reluctance to respond to God's intervention. Peter explained how God led him to go to Cornelius's home and how the Gentiles received the Word regarding the cross, the resurrection, and the forgiveness of sins. Then he described how the Holy Spirit came upon the Gentiles, validating their salvation by faith without the Law. James then went to the Scriptures and reminded the Council that the prophets predicted that one day the Gentiles would be included in Israel (Acts 15:16–17).

The Holy Spirit brought agreement between the apostles and elders, validated by the whole church. The Council of Jerusalem acknowledged what God was doing, obeyed, and wrote to the churches, explaining the decision. God was adding Gentiles to his church through faith, not through the Law, on the same basis that Jews are saved. Acceptance of Gentile believers, without forcing them to submit to the Law, became the new norm.

The Council cleared the way for an unencumbered mission to the Gentiles. God had brought renewal to a missionary movement that was in serious danger of settling down. God had used others like Stephen (Acts 7), Philip (Acts 8), some unnamed believers (Acts 11:19–21), and Paul and Barnabas (Acts 13:46–49) to prepare the way. James, the Lord's brother, representing the traditional Jewish believers, gave his support (Acts 15:13–19). It is clear Peter did not act alone, yet he was chosen by God to ensure the expansion of the Gentile mission did not split the Jewish church.

God intervened to raise the levels of discontent by showing Peter the gap between Jesus' command to make disciples of the nations and the current practice of the church. The Word of God came to Peter, challenging his assumptions, and the Holy Spirit took him on a journey of discovery. God renewed his people on Mission through his Word and the Holy Spirit. The story of Cornelius is the story of three conversions: Peter, Cornelius, and the Jerusalem church. God was the author of each transformation.[18]

Renewal cannot occur without a return to Identity—Word, Spirit, and Mission. But it's not all that needs to happen. It must be an *innovative* return to Identity. Innovation involves a fresh and disciplined application of the characteristics of movement Strategy—Pioneering Leaders, Contagious Relationships, Rapid Mobilization, and Adaptive Methods. Movements in Maturity must turn reluctance into obedience. There's a price to pay—confusion, conflict, and the awkwardness of change. But if that's the cost of turning a movement around, it's worth it.

4. Raise descendants

Movements in Maturity need fresh challenges and new opportunities. They need to have children and grandchildren to make them young again. This happened to the church in the Syrian capital of Antioch.

A group of unnamed disciples who had fled persecution in Jerusalem brought the gospel to Antioch. The message spread to the Jewish community and to Gentiles connected with the synagogue—and from them to their pagan friends and relatives. For the first time, Gentiles were converting to faith in Christ in large numbers (Acts 11:19–26). Some years later, five men from this church at Antioch gathered to fast and to worship the Lord. The Holy Spirit interrupted their gathering to reveal that, after a year of consolidating work at Antioch, it was time for Barnabas and Paul to return to pioneering evangelism and church planting (Acts 13:1–3). Antioch was the first church with a significant mix of Jews and Gentiles. Now this church launched a missionary band that would plant churches in strategic cities across the eastern half of the Roman Empire. Just as Antioch had been the key to reaching Syria, so Philippi became the doorway to Macedonia. The city of Thessalonica was the launch point for both Macedonia and Achaia; Corinth served for the region of Achaia, and Ephesus was the base for reaching Asia Minor.

As missionaries, Paul and Barnabas continued to partner with the church at Antioch and returned to report on progress. In this way the church at Antioch was renewed as it looked beyond its own existence for the multiplication of disciples and churches in other key cities. It became a movement, mobilizing people to act without direct supervision, thus heading toward becoming a great-grandparent—trusting God to give generations of descendants.

LEADERSHIP FAILURE: MATURITY

- **Stumbling over success:** Assuming past achievements will continue into the future.
- **Ignoring the ideal-real gap:** Allowing reality to triumph over the ideal.
- **Choosing extremes:** Choosing between traditionalists (separation from the world) and progressives (peace with the world)—or allowing unresolved conflict between them.

LEADERSHIP TASKS: RETURN TO GROWTH

- **Confront reality:** Restore the tension between the ideal and the real.
- **Seize the opportunity:** Be attentive to God's intervention.
- **Remember who you are:** Retrieve the past and make it serve the present. Align everything with the Word, the Spirit, and the Mission. Apply the characteristics of Strategy in an innovative way.
- **Raise descendants:** Focus on generations of spiritual children, grandchildren, and great-grandchildren.

CONCLUSION

It's not impossible to turn back the clock on the movement lifecycle, but it is hard. As happened with the Quakers, moving from Growth to Maturity and drifting from Maturity to Decline is the normal pattern. It's possible to delay the process for decades, as Methodism did. But once inertia set in, Methodism's breakaway children and grandchildren, such as the Primitive Methodists, kept the vision of John Wesley alive. They too eventually institutionalized, some even reuniting with the parent body before continuing their decline together.

Movements cannot stand still. If the warning signs are not heeded, the contentment of Maturity will yield to the complacency of Decline. Organizational survival replaces the founding cause as the reason for existence, and the movement becomes an inwardly focused institution.

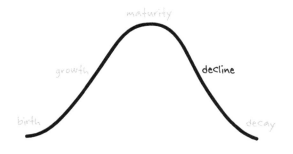

5. DECLINE
SELF-INTEREST RULES

Every great cause begins as a movement, becomes a business, and eventually degenerates into a racket.

—Eric Hoffer[1]

On May 6, 1527, renegade troops of the Imperial army breached the city walls and flooded into Rome, the capital of Christendom for 1,200 years. The looting, fires, rape, and murder raged out of control for days. The occupation lasted nine months. "Only when plague appeared and food vanished, leaving famine, did the drunken satiated hordes recede from the stinking slaughterhouse they had made of Rome."[2]

Pope Clement had relied on Rome's sacred status to protect it. But Rome had become a secular military and political power; it was a traitorous ally in the rivalry between France and the Hapsburg-Spanish Empire. Many believed that the sack of Rome was God's judgment on the sins of the popes and the church hierarchy.[3]

How did this happen? How could church leaders be so out of touch with reality? Decline creeps up on its prey. Powerful institutions, living off the legacy of the past, assume they will continue forever. A movement becomes an institution when it abandons its cause and exists for itself. Protected by dysfunctional bureaucracies, they are shielded from the surrounding world. Declining institutions no longer live for a cause beyond themselves; the one thing that matters is self-preservation. But when disaster strikes, the vulnerability of the institution is laid bare. This is the story of the decline and fall of the church of the Renaissance.

These are the signs of a movement in decline:

1. The world invades the church
2. Centralized power and control
3. Culpable blindness

1. The world invades the church

There were two aspects of the worldliness of the Renaissance popes: one was a secular worldview, the other was their sinful behavior. The two reinforced each other.

As the culture of medieval Europe was being overturned, Christianity was facing a crisis. Those under the sway of the new worldview of the Renaissance were indifferent or antagonistic towards Christianity; they wanted to control the church for their own purposes.[4] The Renaissance was an era in which the secular values of this world replaced the heavenly values of the next. The individual was the master of his fate: "His needs, his ambitions and desires, his pleasures and possessions, his mind, his art, his power, his glory, were the house of life."[5] As vast opportunities opened up for commercial and territorial expansion, European culture and power spread throughout the world.[6]

The Roman Catholic Church was the sole official form of Christianity in Western Europe. Yet its leadership had fallen under the spell of the humanism of the Renaissance. The pope had become a secular prince. These princes of the church outshone the secular princes in their patronage of the arts, worldly pursuits, sexual immorality, extravagant wealth, political intrigue, and selfish ambition.[7] When Cardinal Rodrigo Borgia bought his way into the papacy to become Pope Alexander VI, his character, his mistresses, and his seven children led one observer to exclaim: "Flee, we are in the hands of a wolf!"[8] The church of the Renaissance was a church in decline.

A movement begins to age in Maturity when it protects and enjoys its achievements rather than adding to them. In Decline, aging becomes a settled reality. Movements want to change the world; institutions fear a changing world. Hard decisions are avoided, and opportunities are lost. The leaders wait to respond to circumstances instead of seizing opportunities. Declining movements remember a glorious past but can't deal with the present and future—the assumption is that previous successes will continue, and no one wants to draw attention to ineffective activities. For a while the plan appears to work. In Maturity, when a movement stops being proactive, it doesn't lose effectiveness immediately; there's a lag. The momentum of the past continues to propel the movement forward, but only for a time. In Decline there's nowhere to hide; it becomes obvious that this movement has become a failing institution. As Decline takes hold, self-preservation becomes primary; as the institution loses touch with its reason for existence, survival is everything.

2. Centralized power and control

We have seen how dynamic movements in Growth balance flexibility and control. They are clear about their Identity and release authority and responsibility. In Decline, the institution centralizes power and control.

In the Renaissance, Rome became the center of power and control for Western Christianity. Its glory upheld the faith. On his deathbed in 1455, the first Renaissance Pope, Nicholas V, urged his cardinals to continue the building of Rome. He believed:

> *A faith sustained only by doctrine will never be anything but feeble and vacillating [...] If the authority of the Holy See were visibly displayed in majestic buildings [...] all the world would accept and revere it.*[9]

Throughout the fifteenth century, the papacy consolidated its power over the rest of the church. Power was centralized in the hands of these worldly princes. They created a bureaucracy where positions were bought by the highest bidder.[10]

Declining institutions reward leaders for serving the organization rather than the cause. Formality dominates. People are nice, but little gets done. Those with a financial or emotional attachment to the institution want to preserve it. The institution loses its moral and spiritual authority, and good people leave. Institutionalism is a sickness of the soul. At its heart is the desire for security and control. People give up freedom and responsibility in exchange for predictability and regulation. Dysfunctional bureaucracy is a two-way street—the dependency of followers reflects and reinforces the paternalism of leaders. The price of security is that followers yield sovereignty to those in power. The payoff for the ordinary person is the unspoken promise: "We own you, but don't worry, we will take care of you."[11]

Declining institutions have lost their purpose. They stood for something once. That memory has now faded, and all that is left are the outward forms, not the inner reality. Institutions exist to perpetuate themselves—yet they don't remember why. At its heart, institutionalism is not just an organizational problem, it's a spiritual and moral problem. The only hope is a return to Identity. It requires obedience to God's living Word over the power of the institution, a fresh work of the Holy Spirit, and a return to the mission.

The struggle between Jesus and the Pharisees reveals the clash between movement and institution. The Pharisees wanted to control people's access to God through their rules and regulations: the Pharisees made God predictable, and they were in control. But Jesus trampled on their rules as he revealed a God who forgave the worst of sinners and called them to a righteousness that surpassed that of the Pharisees.

3. Culpable blindness

How could the Catholic Church's leadership be so blind to the looming disaster they created?

Like ancient emperors living behind the walls of a forbidden city, these men were oblivious to the reality of the world around them. They were content. They were free of the tension of the ideal-real gap. They were ignorant of their decline and insensitive to the rising tide of discontent. The system they created was corrupt and "they could not change it because they were part of it, grew out of it, depended on it."[12]

These men assumed that power, status, and wealth made the papacy impregnable. For centuries they protected their position by the Inquisition, the sword of the state, the threat of excommunication, and the stake. Over the years, they lost all moral and spiritual authority: "They possessed no sense of spiritual mission, provided no meaningful religious guidance, performed no moral service for the Christian world."[13] The party was over—and they didn't know it.

For those with eyes to see, the signs were obvious: a revolt was coming. In 1516, Girolamo Alessandro (Papal Nuncio to the Empire) wrote to Pope Leo X to warn of the rising tide of discontent in Germany. Immersed in money, marble, and monuments, Leo was not listening. Within a year the flash-point came through Johann Tetzel, Pope Leo's agent for the sale of indulgences. An indulgence is a reduction of the penance due for confessed sin. The church believed it had the power to grant indulgences from the treasury of the merit of Christ and the saints. In 1476, Pope Sixtus IV ruled that indulgences could be applied to souls in purgatory. People believed they could pay for the salvation of departed relatives. The grace of God was for sale.

When the Dominican monk Johann Tetzel came to a town, he was met by a procession of clergy and townsfolk bearing flags and lighted candles. He brought a money chest and a bag of printed receipts. He would set up shop in the most important church in front of a huge cross. The show began. Tetzel claimed that even if a Christian slept with his mother, "the Holy Father had the power in Heaven and earth to forgive sin." He declared, "as soon as the coin rang in the bowl, the soul for whom it was paid would fly out of Purgatory straight to Heaven."[14]

The sound of coins dropping into Tetzel's money chest awakened Martin Luther to the cause of the Reformation—the day of reckoning had come. Luther wrote his thundering response to the scandal of indulgences—the Ninety-Five Theses—and on October 31, 1517, nailed them to the church door at Wittenberg. Nothing was new in a protest about the abuses of the church; the longing for reformation was widespread, but nothing was done. Luther was different. He refused to accept the ideal-real gap. He fuelled discontent. He acted. A solitary monk stood against the power of church and state and cried, "No more!"

BYPASSED: THE RISE OF NEW MOVEMENTS

New movements arise in response to Decline. They may bring change from within or burst out and form new structures.

Luther didn't start with the failings of the church but with his own failure.[15] He wrestled with God, and as the Word of the gospel transformed him, he sought that same transformation in the life and teaching of the church. He wrote:

> All I have done is to put forth, preach and write the word of God, and apart from this I have done nothing. While I have been sleeping, or drinking Wittenberg beer with my friend Philip and with Amsdorf, it is the word that has done great things.[16]

Luther's confidence in the Word gave him the courage to put his life on the line, as he unleashed the Word to reform the church. He had the assurance this was a work of God and so was able to act courageously, putting aside his own fears.

Luther knew who he was before God and stood against the world until the world shifted.

Long before Luther, Jesus' disciples confronted a declining religious movement. When two fishermen came healing and preaching, the Pharisees and the Sadducees stood in their way (Acts 4:1–31). The Jewish authorities arrested Peter and John and brought them before the Jewish high priest, the rulers, and the elders. Filled with the Holy Spirit, Peter announced that the healing came through the name of Jesus of Nazareth—the same Jesus they had crucified and whom God had raised—and that salvation is found in no one else. These religious leaders saw Peter and John's courage and they could tell these men had been with Jesus, even though they were uneducated. The religious leaders could not deny the miracle, yet they commanded the disciples not to speak in Jesus' name. Peter and John answered: "'Which is right in God's eyes: to listen to you, or to him? You be the judges! As for us, we cannot help speaking about what we have seen and heard'" (Acts 4:19–20). The leaders issued more threats and then released Peter and John.

Peter and John's authority didn't rest on their formal position—it rested on their faithfulness to God's Word and the Holy Spirit. They were pursuing the Mission Jesus gave them. Even though their obedience attracted opposition, they were not afraid because their authority came from their Identity. The disciples were God's plan for the renewal of Israel. At the end of the confrontation, Peter and John returned to the believers, and they all prayed. The Spirit came upon them, and everyone spoke the Word of God boldly (Acts 4:31). The word translated "boldly" means "openly and freely." They were uninhibited in proclaiming God's Word despite the opposition. This confidence, this freedom in speech, this boldness before God, is what it takes to turn around institutions in Decline.

DEALING WITH DECLINE

Is Decline inevitable? It's the recurring pattern of history. Can a declining institution be turned around? Yes, but it's rare. We'll revisit this question in chapter seven on Rebirth. Here are three key thoughts on what it takes to turn around Decline:

1. Stay clear and connected
2. Launch a movement from within
3. Return to Identity

1. Stay clear and connected

Effective leaders in a context of Decline serve a greater cause than just rescuing the institution. They are clear about who they are, while remaining connected with the situation and people in it. Leaders who are clear but disconnected have no influence. Leaders who are connected, but not self-defined, mirror their environment and can't change it.[17]

When confronted by the religious authorities, Peter and John spoke the Word freely and without fear—they were *clear*. They had a non-anxious presence—they were *connected* to the people around them. Although they had no formal position in the system, their naïve honesty shook the very foundations of religious privilege and power. They followed the example Jesus set. They were filled with the Spirit, speaking the Word boldly, pursuing the Mission.

2. Launch a movement from within

Even as the leaders of the nation were plotting his death, Jesus was building a movement of people who wanted to do the will of his Father. People trapped in declining institutions feel powerless. That feeling can be an excuse to do nothing. But there is a way forward, as one English vicar demonstrated. It involved launching a movement from within.

For fifty-four years, evangelical Charles Simeon was the minister of a dysfunctional Anglican church in Cambridge, England. His congregation didn't like him or the gospel he preached. At one point they changed the locks on the church doors and shut him out of his own church building. When he began his ministry in 1782, there were maybe a dozen other evangelical ministers left in the Church of England. He changed that. Without permission and without an official position, he took responsibility, and he did something. Simeon saw the students in this university town of Cambridge as future leaders, and so he formed relationships with them through concentric circles:

i.   The entire student body at Cambridge, many of whom at first ridiculed him.

ii.   Those who accepted his invitation to Conversation Parties where Simeon served tea and took questions.

iii. Students who met after the Conversation Parties and were invited to a weekly sermon class.

iv.   An inner circle of six to eight students who met for supper and reflected on what they had learned that week.

v.   A few who worked with Simeon as interns.[18]

As he got to know them, Simeon recommended students for future leadership as pastors and missionaries. He also recruited evangelical students to Cambridge, and if they couldn't afford tuition, he raised funds for them. Simeon wanted to place evangelicals in growing population centers and centers of influence, so when an important church became available, he would bid for it and then go out and raise the funds to place an evangelical in the pulpit. Some of his graduates became missionaries with the Church Missionary Society that Simeon had founded. "No evangelical Anglican in the early nineteenth century exercised a greater strategic influence on the course of the British missionary movement than did Charles Simeon of Cambridge."[19]

When he began his ministry, there was a handful of evangelical ministers left in the Church of England. When he finished, fifty-four years later, evangelicals led one-third of the churches in England. The vast majority were men influenced by Simeon, including many who had been converted through his influence. He was a man of the Word and a man of prayer. "He rose early each morning to study the Scriptures, and often could be seen pacing the roof above his rooms as he prayed for friends and enemies."[20]

Simeon didn't blame the system; he acted. He didn't wait for permission or funds; he raised the money he needed. Simeon staked his life on the authority of the Word, he prayed, and he trusted God to do the impossible. Two hundred years later, his legacy continues. Today two-thirds of the world's Anglicans trace their origins back to the work of the Church Missionary Society, founded by Charles Simeon.

Simeon's strategy for turning around an institution was to launch a movement that changed the institution from within.

3. Return to Identity

The only way back from Decline to vitality is by returning to the Identity that birthed the movement and by promoting innovative Strategies in a disciplined way. Identity doesn't change (Word, Spirit, and Mission) but Strategy and Methods must be renewed and adapted to new contexts. Dynamic movements preserve their Identity while continually updating and renewing their Strategy and Methods. So movements must promote innovation in Strategy and Methods while maintaining high levels of commitment to Identity. Identity defines the boundaries of the movement which puts it in tension with the values, norms, and beliefs of the surrounding culture.

Movements can err in two equal and opposite ways: they

can surrender their Identity to reduce the tension with the culture (progressives); or they can retain their Identity and treat their Strategy and Methods as equally sacred and unchanging (traditionalists). The key is to maintain the tension.

Decline is the fruit of turning away from who we are in God. Our only hope for renewal is to humbly return to our Identity (Word, Spirit, Mission) and then to apply the key elements of Strategy (Pioneering Leaders, Contagious Relationships, Rapid Mobilization, and Adaptive Methods).

LEADERSHIP FAILURE: DECLINE

- **The world invades the church:** Leaders adopt the values and behaviors of the surrounding culture.
- **Centralized power and control:** Leaders serve the institution and themselves, not the cause. Followers comply.
- **Culpable blindness:** Those in power regard themselves as invulnerable. They lose touch with the world around them.

LEADERSHIP TASKS: DECLINE

- **Stay clear and connected:** Turn around decline by being a leader who is self-defined with a non-anxious presence.
- **Launch a movement from within:** Restore hope for a declining institution by promoting a fresh movement within or alongside.

- **Return to Identity:** Return to Identity, and apply the key elements of Strategy in a fresh and disciplined way.

CONCLUSION

The history of the church is the story of the rise and fall and rise of movements. This is something that Jesus foresaw in his warnings to remain faithful under the pressures of persecution, the cares of this life, and the confusion of false prophets and messiahs. Jesus gave us a Mission and promised us trouble. We should be saddened but not surprised when previously dynamic movements forget their Identity and become declining institutions.

It's rare that a movement in the latter stages of Decline will turn itself around. Decay follows Decline as the movement clings to existence while relying on external life support.

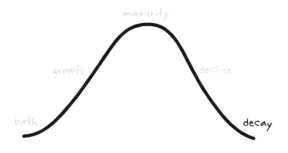

6. DECAY
EXISTENCE ON LIFE SUPPORT

And the Church must be forever building, and always decaying, and always being restored.

—T. S. Eliot

Our world is at war and eternity is at stake. Our enemy is like a roaring lion, seeking someone to devour. Therefore we must be sober-minded and alert (1 Peter 5:8).

We began with Jesus in the wilderness and Satan's attempts to derail his mission and the movement he came to found. It centered on Identity. When Satan had failed in his attempts, he left Jesus, "until an opportune time" (Luke 4:13). He would come back, again and again, when the time was right. The battle never went away until Jesus triumphed at the cross.

Every disciple, and every movement that makes disciples, faces the same relentless challenge from our Adversary. The threat is real. Movements can drift from faithfulness to the Word, the Spirit, and the Mission of God. Whereas a declining institution *drifts* from its Identity, a decaying institution *denies* its Identity.

We all have something to learn from the movements that have risen and yet have stumbled and fallen—not to gain some smug sense of superiority, but to soberly examine our own walk, and to pray that we might be constantly renewed by his Word and the Holy Spirit, remaining faithful to his Mission.

THE EVANGELIZATION OF THE WORLD IN THIS GENERATION

In 1882, the American evangelist D. L. Moody arrived at Cambridge University for a mission, armed only with the gospel. The week began with rowdy crowds of privileged young men mocking this uneducated shoe salesman. The week ended with scores of conversions and seven young men enlisting to join the, then unknown, China Inland Mission, led by Hudson Taylor. These men became known as the Cambridge Seven— men with inherited wealth who were also accomplished sportsmen, and all educated at Cambridge. C. T. Studd, one of the seven, played cricket for England against Australia in the series that began the "Ashes" tradition. He gave away his fortune to become a missionary. It wasn't unusual for prominent evangelicals to support foreign missions, but it was very unusual for them to actually go. Tradesmen, shop-boys, laborers, and apprentices volunteered for missionary service, not gentlemen.[1]

Before they sailed for China, the Cambridge Seven toured England and Scotland, visiting churches and universities and speaking at student rallies. Inspired by their example, university students across Britain volunteered as missionaries. The tour added momentum to the growing national network of evangelical student groups that eventually became the Student Christian Movement (SCM). The student founders of the SCM were evangelicals who accepted "the verbal inspiration of the Bible, the need for a personal relationship with Christ and the importance of missionary work."[2] They adopted as their motto: *The Evangelization of the World in this Generation.*

By 1910, hundreds of former SCM members were serving as missionaries all over the world. The hundreds became thousands.[3]

These are the signs of a movement in decay:

1. From drift to denial
2. Breakdown and collapse
3. Bypassed: The rise of new movements

1. From drift to denial

Despite its success, the Student Christian Movement began to lose its way in the early twentieth century. As the SCM spread to more and more colleges, it broadened its doctrinal base, adopting a liberal Protestant theological stance.[4] The evangelicals within the SCM, and the returning SCM missionaries, were troubled by the movement's drift. In 1910, the Cambridge Christian Union was the first to leave the SCM, and groups from other universities and colleges followed their example.

The SCM took steps to reduce the tension with the culture around them. By 1913, the SCM's statement of faith omitted any mention of the deity of Christ and avoided evangelical terms such as sin, regeneration, forgiveness, and salvation.[5] The SCM leaders claimed it was an attempt to translate Christian concerns into a new language that students could understand.[6] As those leaders rejected the final authority of the Word, they drifted away from faithfulness to the Mission. An internal memo from the SCM missionary secretary in the 1920s complained: "We seem to be sure that all men need to live in a society built upon the teachings of Christ but not at all sure that all men need Christ as the Way to God."[7]

In the case of SCM, the founding generation was under the authority of the Word of God; they experienced God's presence and power through the Holy Spirit as they pursued Christ's call to make disciples of the nations. But by the 1920s, the leaders of the SCM had placed their word above God's Word. They embraced the dominant values of their culture, pulled up their anchor, and drifted. A reckoning came, but not immediately. The SCM went on to establish itself in every university and major college in Britain. By 1957, it had a membership of 7,000 students. SCM leaders played a key role in the founding of the

World Council of Churches (WCC), with former SCM staff and students becoming leaders in the ecumenical movement and in the central bureaucracy of the WCC.[8]

2. Breakdown and collapse

In the 1960s, the Student Christian Movement moved beyond ecumenicalism and liberalism into student radicalism, Marxism, and "Death of God" theology.[9] At the end of the decade, the SCM collapsed. Dutch missiologist Johannes Hoekendijk was influential in the SCM's transformation from a missionary movement to a decaying institution. Hoekendijk regarded the church as an illegitimate center of God's activity, challenging the traditional notion that God was at work in the church to save the world.[10] Instead, he asserted that the secular world was the stage of God's activity: the world sets the agenda for the church.[11]

Hoekendijk became the mentor of those who found signs of God's action in revolutionary political movements, in the anticolonial struggle, and in Marxist ideology.[12] The SCM reinterpreted mission as God's work to end oppression through revolutionary action. Lehtonen observed: "The gospel of the cross is replaced by political and ideological triumphalism."[13] No longer rooted in God's Word, nor led by the Holy Spirit, the SCM bowed to the spirit of the age. The post-war SCM was intent on building bridges to the secular world, ultimately seeking to relieve the tension with the surrounding culture. With the rise of student radicalism this meant:

If the students were not interested in Christianity but were in Marxism then SCM had to build a bridge to the Marxists by showing what a lot they really had in common. If Freudianism was this year's flavor, then SCM had a conference of Christ and Freud. When many young people became attracted to the idea of communal living, [...] the SCM discovered that there was really a strong communal streak in Christianity too and built their own commune.[14]

However, building bridges to the secular world didn't help Marxists become Christians. Instead, Christians became Marxists and left the SCM.[15] The SCM had fallen "under the spell of the increasingly authoritarian political ideologies of the New Left and of neo-Marxism."[16]

By 1973, the movement had practically no student members and was continuing to exist on interest from the financial investment of previous generations.[17] Despite the massive increase in the numbers of students in higher education, the SCM went from 7,000 student members in 1957 to less than 200 by the late 1970s. The SCM survived through the 1980s because capital invested in the 1950s generated the money to pay staff. It had little student support through membership or new financial contributions[18] SCM once had groups on every university and college campus in Britain;

today SCM exists on just twenty-one British campuses. Its work in secondary schools has collapsed, and its publishing arm, SCM Press, has separated.

In 2001, over a century after the Student Christian Movement stood for "The Evangelization of the World in this Generation," its website stated that the SCM "chooses to hold no doctrinal basis" and boasted that membership "is open to people of any faith and none."[19] The original SCM watchword was nowhere to be found. The only motto on the website was *"SCM—Questioning the Christian Faith."*

3. Bypassed: The rise of new movements

By abandoning their Identity (Word, Spirit, and Mission), movements are transformed into religious institutions with weak and vague notions of God.[20] Their decline creates the space in which new movements arise that call God's people back to their Identity. This is the pattern we see repeated in the Bible in the story of Israel. God judged his people, and Isaiah clearly communicates the devastation Israel will endure at God's hand (Isaiah 6:13). John Oswalt comments, "The nation will be like a forest whose stumps are burned after the trees are cut down."[21] Desolation will be complete, but desolation is not the end. God has not finished with Israel, and his promises to bless the nations through his offspring will be remembered. From that stump, a new green shoot will emerge (Isaiah 11:1). Out of judgment comes the hope of renewal. That renewal is always beyond our ability; it is always God who initiates it.

The devastation of God's judgment is never the final word. His purposes will not be overturned by our unfaithfulness. He is faithful and will bring new life. Isaiah looked forward to the coming of the Messiah, the shoot from the burned out stump of Jesse. In contrast to Israel's failed kings, the Messiah would be endowed with the Spirit of God.

The first green shoot that emerged from the SCM was the breakaway evangelical student movement that formed in 1928 as InterVarsity Fellowship, now known as the Universities and Colleges Christian Fellowship (UCCF). The breakaway began with the withdrawal of the Cambridge students—the key university in the establishment of the SCM. Other universities and colleges followed.[22] The UCCF now has 20,000 student members and forty-nine full-time staff in the United Kingdom. It has also reproduced evangelical student movements globally, and in that sense can lay claim to being the modern-day successor to the Cambridge Seven.[23] In recent times, other evangelical student movements have formed on British campuses. The UCCF and these newer movements will be facing the same challenges that diverted the SCM.

A key to the vitality of a movement is its ability to remain both connected and distinct from its environment. Movements like InterVarsity thrive when they remain both connected and distinct. Christian Smith describes this as "engaged orthodoxy."[24] In contrast, Protestant fundamentalism, "is defensively separate from the surrounding culture. It is distinct but not engaged. As a result, fundamentalism is a movement turned in on itself, lacking vitality."[25] The SCM did the opposite: it identified with the dominant political and cultural agendas of its day, but it was not distinct. It mirrored its environment instead of changing it. They traded away their birthright as a missionary movement under the Word and Spirit.

The SCM's mission drift 1880s–1980s

1880s	1980s
Biblical authority	Critical biblical scholarship
Salvation from sin and judgment	Salvation as social and political transformation
A membership of committed Christians	A membership that questions the Christian faith
Christ alone as Savior	Christ fulfilling all religions
Evangelism at the heart of mission	Mission as the kingdom of God in the secular world
Financed by participants	Financed by the investments of previous generations
Biblical and theological studies	Oppressive and authoritarian political ideology
Engagement in world missions	Support of revolutionary movements
The struggle for holiness	The struggle for gay and lesbian rights

THE DEATH WISH OF PROGRESSIVE CHRISTIANITY

The Student Christian Movement is one example of a movement that surrendered to the spirit of the age and drifted from the essentials of the Word, the Spirit, and the Mission. As movements abandon their Identity, they morph into declining religious institutions headed for Decay.

In the nineteenth and twentieth centuries, Protestant liberalism sought to make the Christian faith relevant to modern man. Liberalism elevated human reasoning and experience above the Scriptures so every generation and every individual could interpret the Christian faith for themselves. The working of the Holy Spirit was reinterpreted as God's transformation of society through political and social movements. Mission became the pursuit of heaven on earth rather than obedience to Jesus' command to make disciples of the nations. Theological liberalism is beyond recovery as it recognizes no authority beyond itself.[26] When human experience and reasoning are elevated above the Scripture there can be no hope of correction.

As an attempt to reach modern secular culture, it was a disaster. Liberalism became a halfway house to unbelief. The churches emptied of people, and missionaries came home— why go to the ends of the earth if people's eternal destiny is no longer an issue? Decline is not the best word to describe what happened: the Protestant mainline denominations have collapsed and are decaying.[27] They cannot be renewed because they have abandoned their Identity.

Today, a new generation of evangelicals is ignoring the folly of liberalism and wandering down a similar path. To distinguish them from the old-time liberals, I call this new generation "progressives," but the pattern they are following is much the same. Human experience and reasoning are elevated above God's Word; they believe Christianity must be reinterpreted for the postmodern realities, and consequently core beliefs are ignored or rejected. Mission is redefined as social and political transformation, cultural relevance is embraced at the expense of Christian truth and ethics, dependence on the Holy Spirit is replaced by the spirit of the age. This quest for renewal in the Mission is an attempt to undermine the Identity of God's people. The outcome has, and always will be, self-destruction. But when the Western world abandoned this heritage of morality, Christian progressives fell into line. Postmodernists are not offended by this new form of Christianity, nor are they interested in it. Christian progressives talk about reaching those unreached by traditional churches, but I see no evidence of that happening.

In step with old-time liberalism, the Christian progressives' mission has become about political, economic, and social transformation. There's no reason to seek and to save the lost because they believe nobody is lost. God is not offended by sin; Christ died as an example, not as a sin offering. The belief in Christ on the cross dying for the sins of the world is described as "cosmic child abuse".[28]

What Richard Niebuhr said of liberal Protantism is also

true of its postmodern version: "A God without wrath brought men without sin into a kingdom without judgment through the ministrations of a Christ without a cross."[29] Liberal and progressive Christianity are not just a failure of the intellect; they are a moral and spiritual failure. At the heart of both these streams is an unwillingness to live under the authority of God's Word, in the power of his Spirit, pursuing his Mission. Christianity *does* continue to expand in those parts of the world where a passionate, Spirit-empowered faith is combined with a high view of the authority of God's Word and of Mission as the multiplication of disciples and churches. Right now, the future of Christianity is not found in the postmodern West but among the teeming populations of the developing world.

The patterns we have explored in this chapter are nothing new. There was a recurring cycle of apostasy in the history of Israel revealed in the book of Judges 3–16:

1. The Lord does great works on behalf of his people.
2. Israel forsakes the Lord and provokes him to anger.
3. The Lord delivers the people into the hands of their enemies.
4. The people cry out to God to save them.
5. The Lord raises up a deliverer.[30]

One of the recurring themes in the story of God's people is our forgetfulness. We forget God's great deeds on our behalf.

We forget our Identity. We form gods in our own image and worship them.

As we'll see in Rebirth, these dry bones can live, but they cannot revive themselves. It is a work of God: there is no renewal except by his Word and the Spirit. There can be no renewal without repentance. After rising from the dead, Jesus gathered a defeated, dispirited, failed group of disciples together and for forty days he shaped their Identity as he taught them from his Word, prepared them for the coming of the Spirit in power, and gave them their Mission. This world is passing away. Before we can engage the world in Mission, we must disengage from its ways, submitting to God's ways first and foremost before taking the gospel to the ends of the earth.

LEADERSHIP FAILURE: DECAY

- **From drift to denial:** The declining institution has wandered from its Identity. In Decay the institution denies its Identity as a missionary movement under the Word and the Spirit.

- **Breakdown and collapse:** It experiences a rapid loss of membership, leaving a band of bureaucrats whose beliefs and behavior no longer reflect the movement's origins. The institution exists on artificial life support through asset sales, state support, and funds invested by past generations.

- **Bypassed: The rise of new movements**: New movements arise on the fringe and are rejected by the declining institution; these new movements eventually replace the decaying one.

LEADERSHIP TASKS: DECAY

- **Watch and learn:** Be sober and alert, praying you would be renewed by his Word and the Holy Spirit and remain faithful to his Mission.

CONCLUSION

In Revelation, when the risen Lord writes to the seven churches, he calls each one to repentance. Renewal involves turning away from this world and turning back to God and his ways. But how can a church be renewed if it recognizes no authority higher than itself? What hope is possible if the church places its own word above God's Word or if it exchanges the spirit of the age for the Holy Spirit?

The Lord told the church of Ephesus that unless it repented, its lampstand would be removed: it would cease to be a church of Christ (Revelation 2:5).

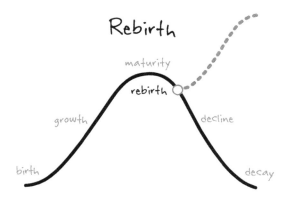

7. REBIRTH
DRY BONES CAN LIVE

*A church which has nothing but the living Word, a church
which is attacked on all sides but has this one defender,
is a church which need not fear for its life, for its youth
is renewed like the eagle's.*

—Visser 't Hooft

Rebirth can occur at any point in Maturity and Decline. The earlier the intervention, the greater the chances of success.

Movements are not reborn through human creativity or design. Rebirth is more than improvement; it is a journey from death to life and is only achieved by returning to the

Word, the Spirit, and the Mission. It is a work of God. In the sixth century BC, Ezekiel learned this lesson. Jerusalem had been overrun, the Temple destroyed, and the people exiled to Babylon. All hope of return and restoration was gone. Then the hand of the Lord came upon Ezekiel, and in a vision, he saw a valley strewn with bones. Bodies denied proper burial. Bones bleached by the sun. This was Israel under the judgment of God. The Lord spoke to Ezekiel: "'Prophesy to these bones and say to them, "Dry bones, hear the word of the LORD!"'" (Ezekiel 37:4). Ezekiel prophesied—and bones were knit back together and covered by flesh and skin. Skeletons became bodies again, but like Adam, the bodies lacked the breath of God and they were still lifeless. The Lord told Ezekiel to prophesy again and "breath entered them; they came to life and stood up on their feet—a vast army" (Ezekiel 37:10).

In Ezekiel's vision of the dry bones, Israel is restored, not replaced. Yet this is a new work of God. It points forward to the coming of the future kingdom of God in the ministry of Jesus. The new reality was also the fulfillment of God's ancient promises to Israel. The new covenant was the rebirth and completion of the old. God promised to give his people a new heart, and put his Spirit in them, so that they would obey him (Ezekiel 36:26–27; Jeremiah 31:31–34). Out of the devastation of judgment came new life as a gift from God.

Plateaued and declining institutions make the mistake of thinking all they need is some reimagining and restructuring. The valley of dry bones teaches us there is no life without the

Word of God, no breath without the Spirit of God, and no direction without the Mission of God.

THE REBIRTH OF JERUSALEM

A century after Ezekiel's vision, God's people are still in exile. The Persians have taken over from the Babylonians as their masters. A Jewish exile called Nehemiah was in Susa, the capital of the Persian Empire, when news came from Jerusalem (Nehemiah 1). Those who survived the exile were in great trouble and distress; the city of David was defenseless, its walls broken down, and its gates destroyed by fire. Nehemiah sat down and wept night and day for days, fasting and praying to God. He prayed to Yahweh, the one true God, who is faithful to the covenant of love that he made with his people Israel, with those who love him and keep his commandments. Israel had not obeyed the commands given through Moses and had broken their covenant. God had therefore scattered them to the nations as he said he would do. Nehemiah confessed the sins of Israel, including himself and his father's family, facing the rightful judgment of God. He didn't make excuses. He didn't blame the Babylonians or the Persians. He confessed his sin and that of his family and his people.

Then he reminded God of his covenant and his promises. Yes, if they were unfaithful, he would scatter them, but if they would return to him and obey him, he would gather them from the farthest horizon and bring them back to Jerusalem, the holy city. Nehemiah faced the judgment of God, which shone a light on the unfaithfulness of God's people. He opened his heart to God in prayer, and drew from the Scriptures the reasons for God's discipline, accepting they were right. Yet those same Scriptures also gave hope that God loves his people and will restore them if they return to him. The God who had judged and scattered could also gather and restore.

The scene ends with this simple statement: "I was cupbearer to the king" (Nehemiah 1:11). So began the amazing story of Nehemiah's return and rebuilding the walls of Jerusalem—and not just the walls, but the renewal of the inhabitants as the covenant people of God.

Nehemiah was a great leader. He aligned everything with a strategy (*how*) and a detailed plan *(what)*. He won the support of the shattered inhabitants of Jerusalem. He formed teams of faith-filled rebuilders and defenders of their city. That's how Nehemiah got the job done and what he did to achieve his goal.

We too want to be like Nehemiah and achieve great things for God. But we forget that Nehemiah's greatness wasn't the starting point of the story. The story begins and ends with the loving, covenant-keeping, Lord of heaven and earth. This is a work of God who called Israel to be a light to the nations. God's discipline was redemptive—he judged his people for their unfaithfulness in order to bring them back to himself. Nehemiah allowed his heart to be moved by God's holy love, responding in repentance. He wept, he prayed and fasted, he cried out to the God who loves his people and who will restore them. This experience shaped Nehemiah's Identity and gave him his *why*.

Nehemiah experienced deep change at the hands of God. Only then did he step onto the stage of history with a strategy and a plan.

These are the three keys to the Rebirth of a movement:

1. Face God's discipline
2. Pursue deep change
3. Realign everything

1. Face God's discipline

A recurring theme in both the Birth and Rebirth of movements is the discipline of God. Founders and re-founders are called out of the fiery furnace of God's testing and discipline. Suffering prepares the way for deep change in Identity. Jesus, tested in the wilderness, is our example: "Son though he was, he learned obedience from what he suffered" (Hebrews 5:8).

Jesus warned his followers that temptations and deceivers would come and seek to draw away even the chosen. Before his departure, Paul warned the Ephesian elders that wolves would arise from within the church, seeking to destroy it. He urged these leaders to be vigilant because of the attacks that will come. In the book of Galatians, he warned the churches that if they succumbed to deception, God would discipline them (Galatians 1:6–9). God's people are prone to go their own way. That's why the judgment of God is at work in the world, and his people are not exempt.[1] Why does God judge his own people? Because God's love is a holy love. Paul writes:

"when we are judged in this way by the Lord, we are being disciplined so that we will not be finally condemned with the world" (1 Corinthians 11:32). His judgments in this life are not final. God disciplines those he loves (Hebrews 12:6). That's why God's judgment begins with his household (1 Peter 4:17).

In Revelation, the church at Ephesus was in grave spiritual danger. Christ reminded the saints of their first love and then rebuked them, saying: "Consider how far you have fallen! Repent and do the things you did at first. If you do not repent, I will come to you and remove your lampstand from its place" (Revelation 2:5). This is a church praised for its orthodoxy but condemned for its loss of passion. The members have purity of belief but no heart to reach a lost world.[2] Christ warned the Ephesians he would remove their lampstand. The church is the lampstand (Revelation 1:20), and God and the Lamb are the lamps (Revelation 21:23–24; 22:5). If the Ephesian church does not respond, the church at Ephesus will be no more; they will no longer be a witness to their world. In G. K. Beale's commentary on Revelation he reminds us: "If Jesus was ready to come in this way to the Ephesian church, He must have come repeatedly throughout history to various churches in similar judgment."[3]

God's discipline extends to individual believers, to churches, to organizations, and to movements that stray from his purposes. That's why rebranding, or restructuring, or marketing, or strategic planning, or spending more money cannot breathe life into a declining movement. Rebirth begins with repentance: it begins with a return to Identity in God's Word, Spirit, and Mission.

A journalist recently asked Anglican archbishop, Justin Welby, about his views on marriage and sexuality. He was unable to give a clear answer on issues that are clear in Scripture and have been the teaching of the church for 2,000 years. He acknowledged: "I haven't got a good answer, and I am not doing that bit of work as well as I would like."[4] Justin Welby is not the only Christian leader caught in a shifting culture, leading a divided denomination. Despite pockets of renewal and orthodoxy, the Anglican church is in danger of serious, long-term decline.[5]

The archbishop is not alone; church leaders across the Western world are struggling. We need a roadmap that takes us back to our Identity as a people obedient to the Word, dependent on the Holy Spirit, and faithful to the Mission, no matter what the cost. If God's Word is supreme, dry bones can live again.

2. Pursue deep change

Rebirth involves a return to Identity. To survive, every living thing is both constantly changing and constantly remaining the same. If an organism doesn't do both, it ceases to exist. Living organisms are continually seeking self-renewal by referring back to their essential Identity and adapting to their environment. Likewise, movements must adapt to their changing environment while remaining true to their Identity.[6]

When declining movements seek change, they often settle for incremental improvements. But what they need is "deep change."[7] Instead they apply rational analysis and careful planning within an existing paradigm. Incremental change does not require that we let go of control. Deep change does. Deep change demands we see the world differently and act according to a new paradigm. It requires something of us: we must surrender control and go on a journey. Deep change requires a shift in our Identity.

In the Old Testament, repentance is the posture of God's people who have experienced his discipline and are trusting him for restoration.[8] The core message of John the Baptist, Jesus, and his disciples was repentance for the forgiveness of sins.[9] True repentance turns away from mindsets and behaviors that damage a relationship with God, and embraces mindsets and behaviors that enhance that relationship.[10] It is always relational—a turning back to God—and is only made possible by God's kindness, mercy, and grace working in our hearts. Repentance is expressed in our desires, words, and actions and is a way of life for a disciple: constant, daily decisions to turn to God and live in obedience to him.

In John 13–17 Jesus prepares his disciples for his departure. Their relationship with him is about to change because he will no longer be physically present with them. How will they continue to relate to him? Jesus declares: "I am the true vine" and urges them to remain in him if they are to be fruitful. Jesus is drawing an image from the Old Testament of Israel, the covenant people of God. Israel was the vine that failed to produce good fruit and faced the judgment of God.[11] Remaining in him involves obedience to his commands, especially the command that disciples love one another (John 15:7–17). By remaining in him, disciples are dependent on Jesus, not their own resources. No branch has life apart from Jesus; our Identity is in him.

Jesus describes how the Father himself prunes every fruitful branch so it will produce more fruit. The disciples have already experienced this pruning, because of Jesus' Word spoken to them. His Word—his teaching, who he is and what he does—is already shaping who they are.[12] The Father cuts off branches that don't bear fruit. He removes the dead wood so that the living, fruit-bearing branches can grow.

Disciples remain in relationship with Jesus by obeying his teaching, and through the coming of the Spirit he remains in them. Then they will "go" and produce fruit that will remain, for love of the Father and the Son cannot be contained (John 15:16).[13] This is the secret of Rebirth, the life of Christ in us, the Gardener who prunes so that we will be even more fruitful. Pruning is painful, but it's necessary for deep change in our Identity. Jesus was preparing these disciples for their greatest failure—they would all run away and leave him. These were hard lessons that shook their confidence in themselves and, for a moment, shattered their faith. At the cross they were broken men, but the risen Lord restored them through the teaching of his Word; and thorough the coming of his mighty

Holy Spirit they were made ready to shoulder the task of their Mission. They knew their limitations and failures; even more, they knew his grace and power.

Movements that return to the Word, the Spirit, and the Mission will find their way to effective Strategy and Methods. The road to Rebirth runs through Identity. That's why deep change often begins in the wilderness, where hard lessons can be learned and transformation can take place.

3. Realign everything

A return to Identity provides the spiritual and moral authority for a fresh look at our Strategy and Methods. It's like we're back in Birth, starting from scratch. But there's an important difference—something already exists that has a history; people are invested in the way things have been done.

Nehemiah was a man of the Spirit, a man of the Word, and a man on a Mission. When faced with dangers, he told his workers to pray *and* carry a weapon. Nehemiah aligned everything with God's purposes; he loved to make lists and delegate tasks; he mastered the important detail; he released authority and responsibility.

Realignment means aligning everything you do with the characteristics of dynamic movements. Simple but hard. Movements are led by Pioneering Leaders who can go into unreached fields, connect, share the gospel, make disciples, form new churches, and multiply leaders. But how do you grow Pioneering Leaders when your existing methods only produce pastor-teachers? Don't begin with a denominational or church-wide restructuring. Don't begin by blaming the leaders you have. Cast vision widely for making disciples. Start training anyone who is willing to learn just enough to get started. Develop the people you see God using. Create a leadership pathway for future Pioneering Leaders. In the next chapter we will look at case studies of how this is already being executed in existing churches.

Rebirth is costly. It takes grace and determination, discipline and time to turn things around. But it can happen. The Rebirth of the Moravian missionary movement is one such example.

THE REBIRTH OF THE MORAVIANS

See what the Moravians have done! Can we not follow their example, and in obedience to our heavenly Master go out into the world and preach the Gospel to the heathen?

—William Carey[14]

Over two hundred years had passed since Martin Luther had nailed his Ninety-five Theses to a church door in Wittenberg. Yet still no significant missionary movement had emerged from the Reformation. But that was about to change. In 1722, a young Austrian nobleman named Count Nikolaus von Zinzendorf opened the doors of his estate in Saxony as a sanctuary for religious refugees.[15] These refugees were Moravian Brethren from the Czech regions of Moravia and Bohemia.

They traced their roots back to the Czech reformer Jan Hus, who had been burned at the stake in 1415. Throughout their history, the Moravians had suffered severe persecution. Their churches were suppressed, and they were hunted down, imprisoned, and tortured for their faith.

On Zinzendorf's estate they built a village and called it Herrnhut (the Lord's Watch). The refugees shared a vision for the rebirth of the church. But instead of birthing the New Jerusalem, the community split into factions in bitter dispute. In response, Zinzendorf moved out of his mansion into the village and served the people. He taught them the Scriptures, reconciled relationships, and restored peace. He appointed leaders based on character and spiritual maturity. He organized the community into bands that met to confess their sins, encourage, and pray for each other. Herrnhut became a place of prayer and worship. Then something amazing happened.

In August 1727, during a week of prayer and fasting, the Moravians experienced an outpouring of the Holy Spirit as they celebrated the Lord's Supper. Their hearts were set on fire with new faith and love toward the Savior and one another. God breathed new life into an ancient movement. Zinzendorf called it the Moravian Pentecost. Herrnhut became alive with days and nights of constant prayer, love feasts, foot washings, festival days, song services, and hymn writing. The Moravians wanted to share their love of the Lamb.[16]

At God's initiative, the Moravians were reborn as a missionary movement. Within twenty years, they had sent out more missionaries than all Protestants combined had sent out in the previous two hundred years. Moravian missionaries were in the Arctic among the Eskimos, in the Caribbean, in South and West Africa, in North America among native Americans, in Suriname, Ceylon, China, India, and Persia. They became the pioneers of the Protestant missionary movement.

Now it's time to revisit the seven characteristics of multiplying movements and see how they apply to the Moravians.

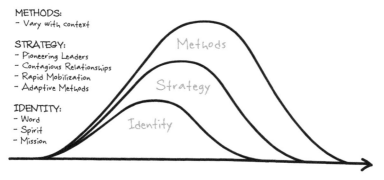

IDENTITY

1. Word—obedient to the Word

Moravian Identity was shaped by a heritage, stretching back to Jan Hus, who stood on the sole authority of God's Word in the life, faith, and mission of the church. For them the Word was to be believed *and* obeyed. This reliance on the Word enabled them to break with the view that the Great Commission had been given solely to the original apostles and had already been fulfilled. At the center of their theology was faith in the atoning sacrifice of Christ for the sins of the world—the only hope for redemption and sanctification.

2. Spirit—dependent on the Holy Spirit

Dispirited and broken, the Moravians were reborn as a movement through the intervention of the Holy Spirit. The Spirit made them aware they were powerless to change themselves. New life through the Spirit led them out of despair and propelled them into obeying the Great Commission. Once on mission, the Spirit was their constant guide and provider where human resources could not sustain.

3. Mission—faithful to the core missionary task

This unlikely group of religious refugees became the first Protestant missionary movement committed to disciple the nations. The focus of their faith and mission was on the sacrifice of the Lamb for the sins of the world. New disciples and churches were the reward for Christ's sufferings. For the first time, whole families were going to the ends of the earth with the gospel. They didn't know how, but they committed themselves to the task and expected God to make a way.

STRATEGY

4. Pioneering Leaders

As a movement pioneer, Zinzendorf embodied what God was doing in the Rebirth of the Moravian movement. He lived out the calling of the movement and inspired others to follow. In their Strategy, Moravians maintained both a distinction and a partnership between the Moravian missionary movement and the churches they planted. They followed Paul's practice of apostolic bands in partnership with local churches.[17]

5. Contagious Relationships

Zinzendorf urged missionaries to follow relational ties in evangelism. He urged them to pray that the Holy Spirit would lead them to people God had prepared. Those who believed were the first fruits. He taught that the stories of the Ethiopian eunuch and Cornelius (Acts 8, 10) showed how to depend on the Holy Spirit to reach these first fruits who would then reach their communities.[18]

6. Rapid Mobilization

These first fruits were baptized, trained, and made responsible to lead the local churches as elders and teachers.[19] The Moravians were trained not to rule over the new believers but to trust the Holy Spirit for spiritual authority. They were to follow Jesus' example of servant leadership, equipping others as local leaders and missionaries. From the beginning, converted African slaves in the West Indies preached and taught the gospel in Creole.

7. Adaptive Methods

At Herrnhut, Zinzendorf prepared the way for renewal through the system of discipleship bands. The rapid expansion of the movement was made possible by a relative lack of concern with training, finances, or organizational structures. In the field, the Moravians had no intention of imposing cultural change—they shared the gospel and expected the Word to do the work. In North America, they translated the Bible into the Delaware and Mohican languages. In Greenland, they used the Inuit language. While the more traditional Protestant groups stayed at home, the Moravians took the gospel to the world and adapted their Methods as they went.

The Rebirth of the Moravians inspired others who followed their example, including William Carey and John Wesley. The result was the birth of missionary movements that changed the world.

LEADERSHIP TASKS: REBIRTH

- **Face God's discipline:** God's judgment prepares the way for Rebirth.
- **Pursue deep change:** Rebirth requires a return to Identity (Word, Spirit, Mission).
- **Realign everything:** Rebirth requires a realignment of Identity and a return to effective, realigned movement Strategies—Pioneering Leaders, Contagious Relationships, Rapid Mobilization, Adaptive Methods.

CONCLUSION

Christianity began the nineteenth century as a European faith. Due to the work and influence of the Moravians, by the end of that century, Christianity was becoming a global movement. Rebirth requires deep change. God's loving discipline prepares the way for repentance and the rediscovery of Identity. God's people surrender again to the authority of his Word in the power of the Holy Spirit. A return to Identity results in a rediscovery of effective movement Strategies and Methods, resulting in the multiplication of disciples and churches.

Rebirth is a gracious work of God, which we cannot engineer. Our call is to respond to God's discipline and partner with him in his Mission. In the next chapter, we'll look at a contemporary example—the emergence of the NoPlaceLeft coalition.

8. NOPLACELEFT
A CASE STUDY

I will not venture to speak of anything except what Christ has accomplished through me in leading the Gentiles to obey God by what I have said and done—by the power of signs and wonders, through the power of the Spirit of God. So from Jerusalem all the way around to Illyricum, I have fully proclaimed the gospel of Christ.

But now that there is no more place for me to work in these regions...

—Paul

NoPlaceLeft is an international coalition of practitioners, churches, and ministries committed to multiplying disciples and streams of reproducing churches across the world. It's a cause they embrace, not an organization they join. Participation is simple: obey the Great Commission. Their name was inspired by Paul's statement that there was "no place left" for him in the eastern half of the Roman Empire (Romans

15:23). Paul had completed his task by establishing streams of reproducing churches. He was ready to move on to Rome and then to Spain to begin the campaign to reach the western half of the empire.

NoPlaceLeft is a new movement that has moved from Birth to Growth. It is also a catalyst for the Rebirth of existing churches and ministries.[1]

NOPLACELEFT BEHIND BARS

Iesus has been in solitary confinement for the last eighteen years. He steps out of his cell, shackled hand and foot. Two guards escort him down a corridor and into a room. As he enters he's overwhelmed by the colors. Iesus lives in a colorless world: the guards wear grey, his cell is grey, prisoners wear white. He never sees color.

Standing by a tub of water is Don Waybright, a mega-church missions pastor in Houston, Texas, and a catalyst for movements behind bars. Don has come to baptize Iesus. As he baptizes Iesus, Don cries out, "Buried with Christ in baptism! Raised to fullness of life in Christ!" Iesus stands up dripping wet, raising his handcuffed hands, and his previously dark and menacing face is covered in innocent joy.

Iesus is an inmate at the Darrington Maximum Security Prison just south of Houston, Texas. In 2013, when Don first started training Darrington inmates in multiplying disciples, he never thought one of the most receptive groups would be the prisoners in solitary. But there has been a movement among inmates in solitary confinement at Darrington. These prisoners spend twenty-three hours a day locked in five by seven feet concrete cells. Discipleship takes place as prisoners shout out to one another from their cells. Inmates have come to Christ just by listening in to these discipleship groups in solitary.

In 2015 four of the men Don trained were transferred to Coffield Prison in East Texas. Coffield is the largest prison in the state with 4,800 inmates. These four men started a program for new disciples who wanted to learn how to multiply disciples and groups in the prison. The program is structured around the five levels of leadership in a multiplying movement.[2] They have 150 inmates just in Level One: Learning how to Obey the Commands of Christ. There's a waiting list to join.

The first command of Jesus they study is "Repent and Believe." The second command is "Be Baptized." After the second lesson, they typically baptize fifty to seventy new believers. African American brothers are baptizing former Aryan Nation (white supremacist) inmates. Mexican inmates have renounced their allegiance to their criminal gangs and risked their lives to be baptized. The inmates at Coffield Prison are not permitted to form churches, but they have formed 225 discipleship groups that function like churches.

The state of Texas has the largest prison population in the United States. What began at Darrington and Coffield is spreading to other prisons in Texas and beyond. Don Waybright, of Sugar Creek Baptist, has been the catalyst for this new thing that God is doing. The church has adopted a NoPlaceLeft vision and has trained 1,500 of their members in the basics of spreading the gospel and making disciples. When the church does short-term mission trips, their people partner with local believers to plant churches. One team has planted a church among women saved out of prostitution in the red-light district of Mumbai, India.

Don had experienced multiplying disciples and churches in far-away fields, but wrestled with how to make it happen back home. Through Jeff Sundell and the NoPlaceLeft coalition Don began to apply the principles and strategies of movements in the local church and in a strategy to reach the city of Houston.

FROM BIRTH TO GROWTH

In 2008, Jeff and Angie Sundell were reviewing their role as missionaries in South Asia.[3] After ten years of work, there were streams of reproducing churches led by Indians and Nepalis. Jeff was out walking and praying when he felt God say something he didn't really want to hear: "I want you back in America. What you've been doing in India, you'll do in the United States." So he and Angie transferred their responsibilities, said their farewells, and moved back home to Bugger Hollow, North Carolina.

The first two years were hard. The Sundells' savings were gone in a few months. Jeff sold second-hand car parts to make ends meet. Angie returned to her career as a librarian.

The Sundells began field-testing the methods they had used in South Asia. They visited homes, offered prayer, shared the gospel, and looked for houses of peace (Luke 10). It was three months before they were invited into a home for a Discovery Bible Study.[4] It was six months before someone put his faith in Christ. After eighteen months, they had new believers being discipled and some church starts, but it was all very fragile and nowhere near multiplication.

Jeff said it was like hoisting all his sails on a still day—no movement for his "boat." He kept asking, "What are we doing here? God, what are you doing?" In the early days of a movement, God shapes the Identity of founders like the Sundells. They fasted and prayed. They went back to the Word and asked the Holy Spirit to teach them how to apply biblical principles in this new mission field. God was testing Jeff's heart. The one thing Jeff knew was that he must reach his sphere of influence—his family, friends, and neighbors—so they would know Christ and follow him.

Jeff and Angie reached out to nearby communities. One day they were in the town of Henrietta, meeting people on the street and getting conversations going. Angie was thinking to herself, "This can't work in America," when a man on his porch called out, "What are you guys doing?"

Angie answered, "We're praying God's blessing for the community. Is there anything we can pray for you?" He invited them up onto his porch to pray. His mother came out and offered them tea and lemonade. Soon they were inside, sitting around the dining room table. Tracy, a neighbor, came over to see what was going on. He claimed to be the toughest man in the county, and he looked it. Later Tracy took the Sundells from door to door along the street introducing them to the other neighbors and telling Jeff and Angie how to pray for them.

At the end of the day, Angie walked away thinking, "Ok, God. You can work here!"

Jeff is a highly relational movement pioneer. In India, he had learned never to do anything alone. He carried this approach into this work in the States, choosing to form partnerships with other practitioners and ministry leaders right from the outset. He invested himself in coalition building and together they worked on the most effective methods, training in teams and meeting for encouragement and peer learning.

Jeff and Angie trained and mobilized people in churches to get out into the community, make disciples, and then train others. They looked for those who were quick to learn and quick to do. Jeff identified seven emerging leaders and made it a priority to invest sixty to ninety days a year in their development. He had a wider group of thirty leaders and invested around thirty days a year in their development. Jeff and Angie were no longer alone.

Meanwhile, God had other people on a similar journey. A national network was forming that would become the NoPlaceLeft coalition. God had tested and shaped Jeff and Angie's hearts. He tested their commitment to follow his call and trust biblical principles for multiplying movements. He'd shown them it was possible to make disciples and plant new churches in America. Then God connected them with others who he had on the same journey.

When I asked Jeff Sundell about the "heart" of NoPlaceLeft, he told me it is about reaching every unengaged, unreached people group and every city in the world.[5] But he wasn't just looking for people who see that big picture. He said the heart of NoPlaceLeft is about caring for our family, neighbors, and friends, and asking if we love them enough to share the gospel and help them become followers of Christ who make disciples. It starts with the people around us. That's the heart of NoPlaceLeft.

NOPLACELEFT AND THE SEVEN CHARACTERISTICS OF MOVEMENTS

Previously we've looked at the components of Identity and Strategy. Together they are the seven characteristics of multiplying movements. Here's how those characteristics are expressed in the NoPlaceLeft coalition.[6]

IDENTITY

1. Word—obedient to the Word

In multiplying movements, discipleship is expressed in obedience to God's Word.

One of my early introductions to NoPlaceLeft was a

twelve-day training event with Bill Smith. We began every day with a simple Discovery Bible Study.[7] We read the text and retold it. We asked, *"What do we learn about God? What do we learn about people? What will we obey?"*

Obedience-oriented discipleship—reading the Bible with others and learning to do what it teaches—is the building block of disciple making movements, including NoPlaceLeft. At the heart of NoPlaceLeft is the call to obey the Word of God. The key text is the Great Commission in which Jesus challenges his disciples to make disciples by teaching them to obey everything he has commanded. Teaching the Word is not enough. Disciples must learn to *obey* it.

Jacob and Keesha Via serve as missionaries in Haiti.[8] One day Jacob shared the gospel with Benna, a young man who collected their trash. Benna wanted to turn to Christ but explained that he was living with his girlfriend and didn't have the right clothes for church. In Haiti people are frequently turned away from churches if they aren't dressed properly or if they are living immoral lives. Jacob told Benna that he and Keesha would start a church in their home and Benna could come dressed any way he wanted. So Benna turned and believed in Jesus. Jacob baptized him and immediately taught him how to share the gospel with his girlfriend and his neighbors. Then they went together to Benna's home and shared. His girlfriend and some neighbors believed and were baptized.

A few months later Benna told Jacob, "I shouldn't be living

with my girlfriend if I'm a disciple. Can I move in with you until we're married?" Now Benna participates in the church at Jacob and Keesha's home and leads the church he planted in his neighborhood. God's Word and the Holy Spirit did their work on Benna's heart. He learned how to obey Christ and immediately taught others how to obey God's Word.

Leadership development is also Word-centered. *How do we enter an unreached community? What is a church? Who can baptize?* are all questions that can be resolved by careful study of the Scriptures.

Sometimes there appears to be a lack of progress in making disciples. A typical response is for NoPlaceLeft teams to fast and pray, read the Gospels and Acts, and then gather to share insights about the way forward. They expect to find answers in the Word. The Bible is a living tool to guide decisions.[9]

When it's time for a group of new disciples to form a church, they work through the functions of church in Acts 2:36–47. They compare those functions to what they are doing and form a plan to bridge the gap between the New Testament pattern and their reality. Then they identify themselves as a new community of believers. When new churches encounter problems, leaders work through the Epistles, looking to apply the lessons for church health.[10] When it's time to choose leaders, they read 1 Timothy 3, discussing together the characteristics of a godly leader, and decide who is ready for leadership. Sometimes the decision is delayed until a person grows into the role.

Every disciple in NoPlaceLeft is in community, searching the Scriptures, not only for what to believe, but for what to do.

2. Spirit—dependent on the Holy Spirit

Every disciple of Jesus has access to the life of God through the Holy Spirit. The same Spirit who came upon Jesus now bestows power and authority upon every disciple to make disciples of the nations (Acts 1:8). The Spirit is present in multiplying movements bearing witness to Jesus.

NoPlaceLeft workers enter an unreached community expecting the Holy Spirit to lead them to a "person or household of peace."[11] When Jesus sent his disciples on mission, he instructed them to look for God-prepared people in each village who would welcome them and their message (Luke 10:1–11). That household would become the doorway into the community. Jesus modeled this approach in his encounter with Zacchaeus (Luke 19:1–10). Jesus told Zacchaeus, "I must stay at your house today." At Zacchaeus' home, Jesus met his family and friends and extended household. By the end of his visit Jesus was able to announce to the community that "salvation has come to this house."[12]

In Canada, Danny Mackay and his team connect with people by offering prayer for healing.[13] They follow Jesus' instruction: "When you enter a town [...] Heal the sick [...] and tell them, 'the Kingdom of God has come near you'" (Luke 10:8–9). To do this, Danny has learned to depend on the Holy Spirit. One day he met Steve, a young man walking as though he was in pain; his neck was bent and his shoulder was stiff. Steve had had an accident at work, causing three fused vertebrae. Medical treatment had been unsuccessful. After hearing Steve's story, Danny prayed for him. Steve thanked him and was about to go when Danny asked him if he felt any change in his body. Steve lifted his arm above his head and discovered he could move it freely. But he still wasn't able to move his neck. He grabbed Danny's hand, placed it on his neck, and asked him to pray. After Danny prayed, Steve turned his head and was rotating his arm when there was a loud pop. He wept as he realized his neck was healed. Danny explained to Steve that this had happened because of Jesus' love for him. Steve opened up about his sin and how unworthy he was. After Danny shared the gospel, Steve turned and believed, and was baptized the next day. His discipleship began.

NoPlaceLeft practitioners believe God answers prayer, but their goal is not just a power encounter or even a prayer of conversion. The goal is baptized disciples, in community, learning to follow Christ.

What happens when the prayer for healing isn't answered? Does that hinder the opportunity to share the gospel? Not normally. Regardless of the outcome, most people are touched by the offer of prayer and are open to hearing about the God who loves them.

The Spirit can work in the lives of people even before we encounter them. Justin and Rachel White were out in their community offering prayer, sharing the gospel, and inviting people to follow Jesus.[14] They met Miguel and Paula, who were from Honduras. For years Miguel had a recurring dream of meeting someone who would speak to him. In the dream, Miguel then took what he was told back to Honduras. Miguel had no idea what this meant, but when he met Justin, he realized this was the man in his dream! Miguel was scared. What was God trying to say to him?

Miguel and Paula agreed to meet up and discover more about the God of the Bible. Justin and Rachel took them through the Discovery Bible Studies from Creation to Restoration. At the end of the series, Miguel and Paula put their faith in Christ and were baptized. A few months later, they joined the team reaching out to the community. In 2017, Justin and Miguel went on a mission trip to Honduras. As Miguel was training his fellow Hondurans, he realized that his dream had become a reality.

You won't find NoPlaceLeft people asking the Holy Spirit for a sign before they will go out and share the gospel. They believe that Jesus has all authority and has already commissioned them to go (Matthew 28:18–20). They go expecting the Holy Spirit to lead them to prepared hearts—the "people of peace" who Jesus referred to in his instructions to his disciples as they went on mission (Luke 10).

Training in skills builds confidence, but what sets people on fire is when they step out in obedience and discover Jesus' presence and power through the Holy Spirit.

3. Mission—faithful to the core missionary task

Multiplying movements like NoPlaceLeft make evangelism, discipleship, and the multiplication of churches their primary mission.

God was troubling Greg Pittman about reaching his community and the nations. Greg was challenged by a call to give up the American dream and live to proclaim the glory of God to the ends of the earth.[15] God was about to shake Cedar Ridge Community Church where Greg was the lead pastor.[16]

Greg shared his vision with the church, and together they committed to making 1,000 new disciples in their community. They wanted their local community to become the training ground for fifty workers for South Asia, but they weren't sure how. The missions pastor, Bryan King, contacted Troy Cooper from NoPlaceLeft, who offered to bring a team to Tulsa to train them.[17]

Troy's goals for the training were to create:

- A local church that is a training and mobilization center with its own training team.
- A local team that does weekly "house of peace" searches.
- 3-Thirds Discipleship groups meeting weekly to work through the Commands of Christ.[18]
- A church that commits to reaching its surrounding community (i.e., the 2,000 homes around where it meets) within two years.

Greg Pittman told his elders and staff, "If we're going to have our people do this, we need to do it ourselves." The elders, staff, and pastors then went into the community looking for houses of peace and found God had prepared the way before them. Church members responded to the challenge by sharing the gospel for the first time with people they knew. One couple, John and Liz, led fifteen of their friends and family to know Christ and subsequently baptized them. Some of these people are now part of a new church led by John and Liz.

Cedar Ridge has three teams searching for houses of peace in the community. The teams visit homes, offer prayer, and look for God-prepared households. Most church members know how to share their story (their testimony) and God's story (the gospel). They are praying daily for loved ones who are far from God. Cedar Ridge believes in "both/and." They have both new believers attending existing congregations, and they have new believers forming into new churches in the community.

The vision to send fifty workers to South Asia is taking shape. Cedar Ridge has designed a residency program to train movement pioneers, where learning takes place in frontline ministry. Volunteers commit seven to ten hours each week over one to two years. They meet as church using a 3-Thirds pattern of discipleship. Each week teams are in the community searching for houses of peace that can become church starts. They are training and mobilizing others. There were thirteen residents in training in 2017; about half are headed for South Asia; the other half will continue to serve in their local community. Residencies differ from traditional discipleship programs, in that every participant is engaged in reaching people in their community, connecting, and sharing the gospel. They are forming disciples into new groups and churches. They follow the example of how Jesus trained his disciples for a global mission. (We'll return to Residencies under "point 6. Rapid Mobilization.")

Local churches are embracing a NoPlaceLeft vision to multiply disciples and churches in their neighborhood, nation, and around the world. They have aligned themselves with God's mission and are already seeing the fruit of transformed lives. An increasing number of those churches have established residencies for developing movement pioneers at home and abroad.

STRATEGY

4. Pioneering Leaders

In multiplying movements, pioneers form missionary bands that become catalysts for evangelism in unreached fields, leading to discipleship and new churches. These bands work in partnership with local churches. Ray Vaughn is an example of a Pioneering Leader. At sixteen, Ray was in jail for the eighth time when someone handed him a Bible.[19] Ray was changed forever by the stories about Jesus, and for the first time, he knew he was loved and forgiven by God. Immediately Ray began to share his story and the gospel story. He was a natural evangelist—and that was the problem. He knew how to lead people to Christ but not how to make disciples. Ray says he had a "firehose" approach to discipling. He would meet a new believer for coffee, discover what the believer's need was, and then dump as much knowledge as he could, hoping something would stick.

Then Ray met Jeff Sundell. Jeff taught him about the power of simplicity. He taught Ray to shift his focus from more knowledge to steps of obedience. Jeff showed him how to help new disciples also make disciples, and Ray applied what Jeff taught him. He went into communities, offering to pray for needs and looking for responsive people. No matter who he met, he offered to pray for them. Jeff's mentoring enabled Ray to move from evangelism to making disciples and forming churches.

Ray is now married to Sara and together they are a team—most days they're out in the harvest and form new disciples into churches. They lead a NoPlaceLeft team that trains and mobilizes workers all over the city of Houston. Each team member represents a network of people and churches engaged in making disciples and reproducing churches.

In 2016, the Houston team set a goal to train 5,000 believers in the city. They turned key churches into hubs with their own local outreach and training teams. Now every week, somewhere in Houston, one hub is offering training.

As the Houston work was developing, Ray was often talking on the phone with Jeff Sundell, sometimes for hours—bouncing ideas, getting input, and being mentored. Ray and

Sara have also built relationships with other NoPlaceLeft practitioners around the U.S. and around the world. They meet up
a few times a year to share progress, to identify where they are
stuck, to get input, and to set goals for the next period. The
team has the vision to reach 10 percent of Houston by planting
32,500 churches. By 2025 they want to start a reproducing
church in each of the 165 zip codes in Houston.[20]

NoPlaceLeft makes space for pioneers who partner with
churches to reach neighborhoods, cities, regions, and nations.
These pioneers do not settle down to lead the churches—they
work with the churches to open up unreached fields. They
maintain both a distinction and partnership between the local
church and the missionary band. Local churches are responsible for reaching their regions in depth. They also partner with
missionary bands to take the gospel into unreached fields.[21]

Within the NoPlaceLeft coalition, partnerships are
forming between local churches and mission agencies who
are pursuing multiplication movements. In partnership with
mission agencies, local churches are simultaneously reaching
their community in depth and preparing future church
planters and cross-cultural missionaries.

5. Contagious Relationships

Jesus taught his disciples to enter an unreached field and look
for God-prepared people who act as bridges to the community.
Face-to-face recruitment among pre-existing relationships
was key to the rapid spread of disciple making movements.

When NoPlaceLeft workers enter an unreached community, they likewise look for God-prepared people of peace who welcome the messenger, the message, and the mission of reaching their world (Luke 10). New disciples are taught how to share their story and God's story, the gospel. Where possible, churches are planted around relational networks. But what does this look like?

Troy Cooper heard that 61 percent of people in their twenties who don't want to go to church would be willing to do a Bible study with a friend.[22] So he and his wife Rachel asked their neighbors, "Is that true? Would you be willing to read the Bible with us?" Two couples said, "Yes!" That was Tuesday night. On Thursday night, fourteen neighbors showed up. Some had never met the Coopers—the two other couples had done the inviting.

The group kept growing, as neighbors invited neighbors. Sally came to know Christ through the studies. She was in a crisis—her husband was having an affair and had left her and the children. As he packed his bag, Sally had told him, "You can leave, but I'll never stop loving you because Jesus will never stop loving me. I'll forgive you because Jesus has forgiven me." Dan left. An hour later he was back, having ended the affair. Overwhelmed by the change in Sally's life, he also wanted to follow Christ. They were baptized together a week later. Word spread throughout the neighborhood of what God had done, and the original group became four groups.

NoPlaceLeft workers know that Contagious Relationships

are vital for the spread of the gospel. Once they've found a person of peace, they immediately encourage them to share what God has done with friends and family. They don't extract new disciples from their relationships and place them in a Christian bubble. They get new believers to draw a relationship map of the people they know who are far from God, pray daily for them, and share with them. NoPlaceLeft workers treat every new believer as a disciple maker.

6. Rapid Mobilization

In a multiplying movement every disciple is ordained for ministry. Every disciple is responsible to make disciples. There are no extra-biblical requirements for leadership. Workers are mobilized through a simple pattern called MAWL—Model, Assist, Watch, and Leave.

Kumar Pillai was from a high-caste Hindu family of temple builders in North India.[23] While still a young teenager, Kumar had to take up priestly duties when his father died. Jesus made himself known to Kumar through visions, and, despite his family's opposition, at seventeen he broke from Hinduism and became a follower of Jesus. Rejected by his family, Kumar provided for himself by becoming a mathematics tutor. When other students returned to their homes during vacations, Kumar would go into the countryside of West Bengal and Sikkim to plant churches. When he had led enough people to Christ in an area, he would find a piece of land and build a church for them. Half his income was spent planting churches.

Kumar set a goal before God—one hundred new churches by 2020. By 2007 Kumar had planted eleven new churches. He had just thirteen years left to plant another eighty-nine. For six months he prayed, asking God to either release him from his commitment or show him how he could achieve it. Then Kumar met Nathan Shank, an American missionary.

Through Nathan's training, Kumar realized he was planting churches that remained dependent on him. Kumar saw that multiplication would not happen unless he trained new believers to share the gospel, make disciples, and form new churches that were not reliant on him. Kumar tried this new plan, visiting 300 homes in his neighborhood. He led fourteen men and their families to Christ and then told them he would teach them how to make disciples and plant churches. He met with them and worked through foundational discipleship using the Commands of Christ.[24] He taught them how to share the gospel, how to train disciples, and how to plant churches. Everything he taught them, he practiced with them. Then he sent them out. After three months his trainees had planted one hundred new churches. Kumar had reached his goal, twelve years ahead of time.

The following year he challenged the new churches to plant three churches each. Just over a year later, the network of one hundred churches had grown to over 400 churches. Today there are over 50,000 baptized disciples in multiple networks of reproducing churches across North India.

Kumar has helped others spark multiplying movements in

twenty-five states of India. He trains and coaches movement pioneers in Nepal, Bhutan, Burma, Sri Lanka, Bangladesh, Thailand, Laos, Vietnam, Cambodia, China, and Taiwan. He has challenged each team to reach their own nation and three to four other nations. "Reaching" means there are multiple streams of four generations of disciples and churches. Kumar's vision is to reach ten million people and plant one million churches by 2020.

Kumar's relationship with Nathan Shank was key to his transition from adding new churches to multiplying them. Nathan applied the pattern of Model, Assist, Watch, and Leave. Kumar did the same with the leaders he developed. Those leaders followed the same pattern. Mobilization is rapid because movements are held together by intentional mentoring relationships.

A NoPlaceLeft vision can only be achieved by applying a strategy of Rapid Mobilization. Local church residencies for training movement pioneers are one method that facilitates Rapid Mobilization. Volunteers give at least seven hours each week over twelve months.

The residency weekly rhythm is as follows:

- Three hours in 3-Thirds group discipleship.
- Two hours in the community searching for houses of peace.
- Two hours of training and mobilizing others.[25]

Justin White had thirty participants in his third year of facilitating residencies in Raleigh, NC. He is expecting the numbers to double in the next year. Twenty other residencies were running across the United States, and the first residency program has launched in the United Kingdom. Justin plans to train 300 units (singles and couples) through residencies each year for domestic and global missions.

NoPlaceLeft workers are building a Great Commission pipeline by partnering with churches around the world to reach their local communities, while concurrently identifying and training workers who will go to the nations, supported by their churches.

This is what movements do. They provide multiple on-ramps for leadership development and deployment. They rapidly mobilize even the newest believers. Workers learn on-the-job over the whole course of their life and ministry. Residencies are a game changer in helping to achieve this.

7. Adaptive Methods

Residencies are just one example of a NoPlaceLeft Adaptive Method.[26] Movements that multiply disciples and churches have simple but powerful Adaptive Methods to equip every believer to share the gospel, make disciples, form new churches, and multiply leaders.

The 3-Circles is a simple method for sharing the gospel.[27] You can learn it in a session, practice it, and immediately share it. All you need is a pen and a napkin or other piece of paper to draw on. The impact is immediate. I trained an Anglican church planter in England how to share the 3-Circles. Three days later he rang back to tell me he'd led a couple to Christ who had asked him to baptize their child. Here was a church planter who had been theologically trained but hadn't been leading people to Christ. No one had trained him in the basics. He didn't know how to train his people. A one-hour session changed all that. Now there's a steady stream of people coming to know Christ in that church and moving into discipleship.

Sometimes all it takes is a simple method. When I train people in the 3-Circles, I tell them, "This method doesn't work! The gospel works and the 3-Circles is just one way to explain the gospel." Malachi Cooper, the son of a NoPlaceLeft leader, taught me this method when he was ten years old. He's a teen-ager now, and he's led adults to Christ using the 3-Circles. Now I teach others what Malachi taught me.

Another Adaptive Method is called 3-Thirds Discipleship:[28]

1. *First third*: Share how you've been. Experience mutual accountability for what you agreed to do in the last meeting. Pray and worship.
2. *Second third*: Learn from God's Word using the Discovery Bible Study method.
3. *Final third*: Ask each other, "How will you obey what you've learned? Who will you share with this week?" Pray for each other.

The 3-Thirds is a simple but powerful process for discipleship in groups that anyone can lead. You can learn this method of discipleship in one session. The newest and youngest believers can help facilitate a group. 3-Thirds groups meet in elementary schools, in homes, in cafés, and in prisons around the world. The process works well with corporate executives in New York and with semi-literate villagers in Nepal. If you ask disciples what God has said to them through the biblical text and what they need to do in the coming week, they'll know how to answer. They'll also know how to lead the group without you.

Another example of a NoPlaceLeft Adaptive Method is the Great Commission Pipeline. These Pipelines can begin in any local community and flow to the ends of the earth.[29] There are three stages in the process: *teams, coalitions, and hubs.*

Teams

In partnership with local churches, movement catalysts (experienced practitioners and trainers) provide repeated training in a city to establish teams that pursue the NoPlaceLeft vision. Training equips believers in the basics of sharing the gospel, making disciples, and forming new groups and churches. Where possible, training is local church-based. The goal of training is to form local teams that are in the harvest weekly, are doing 3-Thirds discipleship, and are training and mobilizing others.

Coalitions

The strategy in each location is to establish multiple teams in a coalition pursuing NoPlaceLeft. Movement catalysts partner with teams to deliver training throughout the city. They coach and equip emerging leaders who then take responsibility to reach their city in depth. Residencies are formed to provide leadership development.

Hubs

Movement catalysts work with city coalitions to help them become sending hubs that open up new locations. Churches send short-term teams and deploy long-term workers nationally, cross-culturally, internationally, and among unreached people groups.

Wherever these NoPlaceLeft workers go, they establish teams, coalitions, hubs, and residencies. This strategy has been emerging over the last few years, and there are now hundreds of teams across the United States, dozens of coalitions, five hubs, and twenty residencies. The same strategy is being implemented globally, so believers in traditionally receiving nations are now establishing their own teams, coalitions, and hubs. They are taking responsibility for reaching their nation, unreached people groups, and the ends of the earth.

The Great Commission Pipeline is not just someone's great idea. It's already a reality.

CONCLUSION

I visited the Sundells in the summer of 2018 at their home in Bugger Hollow. They had just flown in from a three-month mission to migrants in Athens, Greece. Metropolitan Athens has a population of 3.8 million. At least one in four people is an immigrant—Arabs fleeing the civil war in Syria, Persians escaping from Iran and Afghanistan, Africans looking for a better life in Europe. Jeff and Angie were working alongside teams in Athens to reach and disciple these migrants and equip them to be church planters as they move on through Europe. Some disciples are even turning around to go back home and reach their friends and families. Many people view migrants as a problem: NoPlaceLeft sees new disciples and church planters for Europe and the Muslim world.

Soon after, the Sundells announced they were going back to the mission field. This time Athens, Greece. Ray and Sara Vaughn have handed over the work in Houston and are also headed for Athens as that city becomes a hub for reaching Europe and the Middle East. Other NoPlaceLeft couples who began in U.S. cities have handed over leadership and are heading out to some of the least reached nations in the world. The work of NoPlaceLeft continues to grow and multiply as they seek to utilize effective patterns of ministry built on a foundational Identity of Word, Spirit, and Mission.

BACK TO THE BEGINNING

As we close, my thoughts return to where we began, with Jesus at his baptism and in his wilderness testing. These two stories mark the birth of the movement he started. They reveal the Identity he wants us to share: his loving relationship with the Father, demonstrated by obedience to the living Word; his reliance on the Spirit's power and guidance; his determination to fulfill his Mission. These are affirmed at his baptism and tested in the wilderness.

In the wilderness there are no disciples, no opponents, no crowds. Just the silence of the desert and the presence of pure evil goading him to deny his Identity. Jesus knows *who* he is, he knows *how* he will fulfill his task, he knows *what* he will do: the world is waiting.

Jesus returned to Galilee in the power of the Spirit and news about him spread everywhere. That day, Jesus launched a missionary movement. The news about him continues to spread down through time and around the world.

As we move forward, we must continually return to be with Christ in his baptism and desert ordeal. Let's recall the disciples as Jesus found them after he had risen: they were done; the movement was over; its terrified leaders locked themselves in a room and shut out the world (John 20:19). The Jesus movement had risen and fallen within just a few years.

What did Jesus do? He brought them back to their Identity. He opened up the Scriptures to them and taught them from the Word of God (Luke 24:27, 45). He prepared them for the coming of the Holy Spirit in power (Acts 1:4–5). He explained their Mission, instructing them to go to the nations with the gospel of the forgiveness of sins, baptizing and teaching disciples to obey his commands, and forming them into churches. They were not to stop until he returns in glory (Matthew 28:16–20; Luke 24:45–49; Acts 1:1–8). The movement was reborn by a return to its Identity. Now it was ready for action.

For as long as you live and serve the Lord, you must never tire of returning to your Identity—the Word, the Spirit, the Mission. Jesus began the movement. He still leads the way.

There's a job to be done and you have a part to play.

What will you do next?

APPENDIX
NOPLACELEFT STRATEGY AND METHODS

The 4-Fields

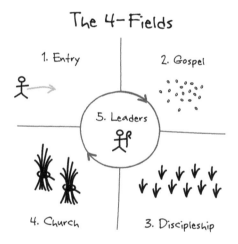

1. Entry   2. Gospel

5. Leaders

4. Church   3. Discipleship

A. NOPLACELEFT STRATEGY

The 4-Fields answers five questions:

1. Entry: How do I enter a new field?
2. Gospel: What do I say?
3. Discipleship: How do I make disciples?
4. Church: How will I form healthy churches?
5. Leaders: How do I multiply leaders?[1]

Go to: www.movements.net/4fields

B. NOPLACELEFT METHODS

Below are some of the most common Methods in use by NoPlaceLeft practitioners as they apply the 4-Fields Strategy.

1. Entry: How do I enter a new field?

Oikos mapping

Oikos is a New Testament word for a household that could include extended family and servants. In oikos mapping, participants identify people in their world who are far from God. They make a list of five of those people and commit to pray for them every day. They share their story and the gospel story with them.

House of Peace search

The House of Peace search equips workers to enter a field where they have no pre-existing relationships and find a God-prepared household of peace (Luke 10:1–11) that links the messenger and the message with the community.

Go to: www.movements.net/1-entry

2. Gospel: What do I say?

The most common gospel outline used is the 3-Circles.[2]

Outline

The 3-Circles

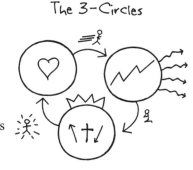

- We live in a broken world.
- God loves us and has a plan for our lives.
- We've gone our own way.
- We try and escape brokenness in various ways. We end up more broken.
- God sent Jesus into the world to show us what God is like and how we should live.
- Evil men crucified him.
- Three days later God raised Jesus from the dead showing his death paid the penalty for our sin and made us right with God.
- God calls us to turn back to him, put our full confidence in Jesus' death and resurrection and make him our King.
- If we do that, God makes us new and puts his Spirit into our lives to change us from the inside out.

Questions

- Where are you in this drawing?
- Where would you like to be?
- Is there anything that would stop you from turning and believing today?

Go to: www.movements.net/2-gospel

3. Discipleship: How do I make disciples?

The 411

This training answers **four** questions, on **one** sheet of paper, in **one** hour (411):

1. Why do we make disciples?
2. Who do we reach?
3. What do we say?
4. When will we do it?

The Commands of Christ

The Commands of Christ are Discovery Bible Studies for initial discipleship. They use the 3-Thirds process below as the pattern of learning:

1. Repent and Believe: A Sinful Woman (Luke 7:36–50)
2. Be Baptized: The Ethiopian Eunuch (Acts 8:26–39)
3. Pray: The Lord's Prayer (Matthew 6:9–13)
4. Make Disciples: The Samaritan Woman (John 4:4–42)
5. Love: The Good Samaritan (Luke 10:25–37)
6. Worship: Paul and Silas (Acts 16:25–34)
7. Celebrate: Lord's Supper (Luke 22:7–20; 1 Corinthians 11:23–29)
8. Give: The Generous Widow (Mark 12:41–44)
9. Gather: The First Church (Acts 2:36–47)

Ongoing discipleship involves either book-by-book or thematic studies of the Scriptures using the 3-Thirds process.

3-Thirds Discipleship

This is the building block for discipleship in NoPlaceLeft. The pattern is applied to disciple pre-believers, new disciples, maturing disciples, and leaders.

First Third	Second Third	Final Third
1. Mutual care	5. New lesson	7. Set goals
2. Worship	Discovery Bible Study • Read the text and retell it in your own words. • What does the passage teach us about God? • What does it teach us about people? • Is there a command to obey or an example to follow? And/or a new skill	• How will you obey what you've learned? • Who could you share with?
3. Loving accountability • Have you done what you committed to do last time?	6. Practice the new learning	8. Commissioning and prayer
4. Vision		

Go to: www.movements.net/3-disciples

4. Church: How will I form healthy churches?

Church Circle

Disciples identify the characteristics of a healthy church (Acts 2:36–47). They place a symbol within the circle if they are fulfilling that function. The symbol is outside the circle if they are not displaying that function. A dotted circle represents a discipleship group that has not yet committed to be church together. A solid line shows the group has committed to be a church.[3]

The Church Circle – Acts 2:36–47

	Those who repent and believe are added to the church		Regular celebration of the Lord's Supper
	Disciples are baptized and have the authority to baptize		Giving to those in need and for the spread of the gospel
	Prayer: Corporate and individual prayer		Learning obedience to God's Word
	Disciples are trained to share the gospel		Recognized local leaders
	Love for one another expressed in deeds		A dotted line circle indicates a group. A solid circle indicates the group identifies as a church
	Worship: Corporate and individual worship		

Go to: www.movements.net/4-church

5. Leaders: How do I multiply leaders?

MAWL (Model, Assist, Watch, Leave)

In each of the 4 Fields, leaders are developed and multiplied by applying a MAWL approach:

1. Model: I demonstrate.
2. Assist: I help you do as you Model for others.
3. Watch: I watch you as you Assist someone to Model.
4. Leave: I create the space so you can take full responsibility.

3-Touch Training for Churches

These are three identical local church training events held two to three months apart. Each event is followed by the rollout of 3-Thirds discipleship groups and a House of Peace search team. By the third event, the local church can run the training itself.

Mid-Level Training

This is a one to two-day event for workers who have done training and are already implementing the principles. It incorporates an "iron-on-iron" segment in which teams and individuals report in, identify where they are stuck, and make new plans.

Generational Mapping

Participants gauge the health of their church, starting with the Church Circle tool and identify any generations of new churches.

4-Fields Intensive

This is three to four days of training that covers biblical foundations and skills across each of the 4-Fields and leadership development.

Residencies

Residencies are connected with a local church or a mission team. They equip future church planters and cross-cultural workers. Participants make a commitment of 7–10 hours a week:

1. Teams meet for church and discipleship in a 3-Thirds format.
2. Every week the teams are in the community looking for houses of peace and establishing groups for discipleship and church formation.
3. These teams train and mobilize others.

Great Commission Pipeline

These pipelines are built by churches that complete the 411 training, establish local house of peace search teams, and host a residency. Over two to three years, they identify faithful and fruitful workers. These proven workers go out to plant churches in the community, around the nation, and among unreached people groups. Wherever they go, they establish local churches that build Great Commission Pipelines.

5-Levels of Leadership

NoPlaceLeft builds leadership at each level of a multiplying movement.[4]

1. Seed-Sower: A disciple who shares the gospel.
2. Church Planter: A Seed-Sower who learns how to make disciples and plant churches.
3. Church Multiplier: A Church Planter who learns how to start churches that reproduce generations of new disciples and churches.
4. Multiplication Trainer: Church Multiplier who learns how to equip other church multipliers to achieve third and fourth-generation churches.
5. Movement Catalyst: A Multiplication Trainer who takes on a broad responsibility to reach an unreached population segment or region.

Go to: www.movements.net/5-leaders

The 5-Levels of Leadership

	L1 Seed Sower	L2 Church Planter	L3 Church Multiplier	L4 Multiplication Trainer	L5 Movement Catalyst
			← Addition ┊ Multiplication →		

A disciple who
- spreads the gospel among family and friends
- masters simple, effective tools for sharing the gospel
- loves lost people
- models seed sowing to others

A level 1 leader who
- learns how to make disciples and plant churches
- trains level 1 workers to share the gospel
- forms disciples into groups that become churches

A level 2 leader who
- starts churches that reproduce churches to four generations
- equips level 1 and level 2 leaders
- ensures the health of churches and releases authority to local leaders

A level 3 leader who
- produces four generations of new churches across multiple streams of church planting
- engages beyond the leader's own network to cast vision and train for multiplication
- identifies and resolves barriers to multiplication

A level 4 leader who
- becomes a catalyst for multiple streams of church planting among unreached people groups
- equips level 3 and level 4 leaders to facilitate multiple streams of multiple generations of church planting
- majors in networking, resourcing and vision casting

BIBLIOGRAPHY

Addison, Steve. "Missionaries to Marxists: The Rise and Fall of SCM"[blog]. *Movements*, August 15, 2006. https://www.movements.net/blog/2006/08/15/missionaries-to-marxists.html . Accessed January 15, 2019.

————. *Movements That Change the World: Five Keys to Spreading the Gospel.* Rev., Downers Grove, IL: InterVarsity Press, 2011.

————. *Pioneering Movements: Leadership That Multiplies Disciples and Churches.* Downers Grove, IL: InterVarsity Press, 2015.

————. *What Jesus Started: Joining the Movement, Changing the World.* Downers Grove, IL: InterVarsity Press, 2012.

Adizes, Ichak. *Corporate Lifecycles: How and Why Corporations Grow and Die and What to Do About It.* 4th edn. Englewood Cliffs, NJ: Prentice Hall, 1998.

————. *Managing Corporate Lifecycles.* Paramus, NJ: Prentice Hall Press, 1999.

————. *Mastering Change: The Power of Mutual Trust and Respect In Personal Life, Family Life, Business and Society.* Santa Barbara, CA: The Adizes Institute, 1992.

——. "Organizational Passages—Diagnosing and Treating Lifecycle Problems of Organizations." *Organizational Dynamics* 8/1 (1979).

——. *The Pursuit of Prime: Maximize Your Company's Success With the Adizes Program*. Santa Monica, CA: Knowledge Exchange, 1996.

Allen, Roland. *The Spontaneous Expansion of the Church: and the Causes which hinder it*. 3rd edn. London: World Dominion Press, 1956.

Bainton, Roland H. *Here I Stand: A Life of Martin Luther*. Nashville: Abingdon, 1950.

Baker, Frank. *From Wesley to Asbury: Studies in Early American Methodism*. Durham, NC: Duke University Press, 1976.

Beale, G. K. and D.H Campbell. *Revelation: A Shorter Commentary*. Grand Rapids: Eerdmans, 2015.

Bell, Rob and Doug Pagitt. "Rob Bell and Doug talk about What Is The Bible?" [video]. YouTube, recorded April 2. www.youtube.com/watch?v=w50q4UZlUMQ . Accessed December 15, 2017.

Bennett, John C. "Charles Simeon and the Evangelical Anglican Missionary Movement—A Study of Voluntarism and Church-Mission Tensions." PhD thesis, University of Edinburgh, 1992.

Block, Peter. *Stewardship: Choosing Service Over Self-Interest*. San Francisco: Berrett-Koehler Publishers, 1993.

Boda, Mark J. *Return to Me: A Biblical Theology of Repentance*. In D. A. Carson ed., New Studies in Biblical Theology. Downers Grove, IL: InterVarsity Press, 2015.

Boer, Harry R. *Pentecost and Missions*. Grand Rapids: Eerdmans, 1961.

Boyd, Robin. *The Witness of the Student Christian Movement: 'Church Ahead of the Church.'* London: SPCK, 2007.

Braithwaite, William Charles. *The Second Period of Quakerism*. 2nd edn. Cambridge: Cambridge University Press, 1961.

Bruce, Steve. *Firm in the Faith*. Aldershot, UK: Gower, 1984.

———. "The Student Christian Movement: A Nineteenth Century Movement and Its Vicissitudes." *International Journal of Sociology and Social Policy* 2/1 (1982).

———. "The Student Christian Movement and the Inter-Varsity Fellowship: A Sociological Study of Two Student Movements." University of Stirling, 1980. http://hdl.handle.net/1893/2398 . Accessed July 4, 2018.

Cada, Lawrence. *Shaping the Coming Age of Religious Life*. New York: Seabury Press, 1979.

Carson, D. A. *The Gospel According to John*. The Pillar New Testament Commentary. Grand Rapids, MI: Eerdmans, 1991.

———. "Matthew." In Frank E. Gaebelein ed., *The Expositor's Bible Commentary, Vol.8*. Grand Rapids, MI: Zondervan, 1984.

Chalke, Steve and Alan Mann. *The Lost Message of Jesus*. Grand Rapids, MI: Zondervan, 2004.

Chesterton, G. K. *Saint Francis of Assisi*. London: Hodder & Stoughton, 1914.

Clinton, Robert J. *Focused Lives: Inspirational Life Changing Lessons from Eight Effective Christian Leaders Who Finished Well*. Altadena: Barnabas Publishers, 1995.

Collins, Jim. *How the Mighty Fall: And Why Some Companies Never Give In*. London: Random House, 2009.

Conger, Jay A. and Rabindra N. Kanungo. "Behavioral Dimensions of Charismatic Leadership." In *Charismatic Leadership: The Elusive Factor in Organizational Effective ness*. San Francisco: Jossey-Bass, 1988.

Cooper, Troy, "4Fields Discovery: Gospels and Acts" [video]. *Movements*. https://www.movements.net/training-timo thys . Accessed March 12, 2018.

————. "112-Churches Pioneering Movements in Tulsa" [podcast]. *Movements*, April 10, 2016. https://www. movements.net/blog/2016/04/10/112-churches-pio neering-movements-in-tulsa-troy-cooper.html . Accessed February 21, 2018.

————. "Bi-Vocational Weekly Rhythm" [video]. *Movements*. https://www.movements.net/training-timothys . Accessed March 12, 2018.

————. "Church Circles Discovery: Epistles" [video]. *Movements*. https://www.movements.net/training-timothys . Accessed March 12, 2018.

————. "The Great Commission Pipeline" [including video], *Movements*, April 9, 2018. https://www.movements. net/blog/blog/2018/4/8/the-great-commission-pipeline . Accessed April 9, 2018.

Coser, Lewis A. *The Functions of Social Conflict*. London: Routledge & Kegan Paul, 1956.

Cragg, Gerald R., ed. *The Works of John Wesley, Vol. 11: The Appeals to Men of Reason and Religion and Certain Related Open Letters*. Nashville, TN: Abingdon Press, 1987.

Cundell, Arthur E. *Judges and Ruth: An Introduction and Commentary.* In D.J. Wiseman ed., Tyndale Old Testament Commentaries. London: InterVarsity Press, 1968.

Ebeling, Gerhard. *Luther: An Introduction to His Thought,* R.A. Wilson trans. London and Glasgow: Collins, 1970.

Eliot, T. S. *Christianity and Culture: The Idea of a Christian Society and Notes Towards the Definition of Culture.* San Diego: Harcourt Brace & Company, 1939.

Estep, William Roscoe. *The Anabaptist Story.* 2nd edn. Grand Rapids: Eerdmans, 1975.

Ferdinando, Keith. "Mission: A Problem of Definition." *Themelios* 33/1 (2008).

Finke, Roger. "Innovative Returns to Tradition: Using Core Teachings as the Foundation for Innovative Accommodation." *Journal for the Scientific Study of Religion* 43/1 (March 2004).

Finke, Roger and Rodney Stark. "How the Upstart Sects Won America: 1776–1850." *Journal for the Scientific Study of Religion* 28/1 (1989).

Fletcher, Richard. *The Conversion of Europe: From Paganism to Christianity, 371–1386 AD.* London: Fontana Press, 1997.

Fox, George. "Autobiography of George Fox." http://www.ccel.org/ccel/fox_g/autobio.pdf . Accessed August 16, 2017.

Frame, John M. *The Doctrine of the Word of God.* Phillipsburg, NJ: P & R Publishing, 2010.

Friedman, Edwin H. *A Failure of Nerve: Leadership in the Age of the Quick Fix.* New York: Seabury Books, 2007.

———. *Generation to Generation: Family Process in Church and Synagogue*. New York: The Guilford Press, 1985.

Gallagher, Robert L. "The Integration of Mission Theology and Practice: Zinzendorf and the Early Moravians." *Mission Studies* 25 (2008).

Garrison, David. *A Wind in The House of Islam: How God is Drawing Muslims Around the World to Faith in Jesus Christ*. Monument, CO: WIGTake Resources, 2014.

———. *Church Planting Movements: How God Is Redeeming a Lost World*. Midlothian VA: WIGTake Resources, 2004.

Gerlach, Luther P. and Virginia H. Hine. *People, Power, Change: Movements of Social Transformation*. Indianapolis: The Bobbs-Merrill Company, 1970.

Gilbart-Smith, Mike. "Book Review: The Lost Message of Jesus, by Steve Chalke." March 5, 2010. https://www.9marks.org/review/lost-message-jesus-steve-chalke . Accessed February 27, 2019.

Gledhill, Ruth. "Massive Collapse in Number of Anglicans in Britain, New Survey Shows." *Christian Today*, September 4, 2017. https://www.christiantoday.com/article/massive.collapse.in.number.of.anglicans.in.britain.new.survey.shows/113016.htm . Accessed November 7, 2017.

Hatch, Nathan O. "The Puzzle of American Methodism." *Church History* 63/2 (June 1994).

Heitzenrater, Richard P. *Wesley and the People Called Methodists*. 2nd edn. Nashville, TN: Abingdon Press, 1995.

Hempton, David. *Methodism: Empire of the Spirit*. New Haven: Yale University Press, 2005.

Hillerbrand, Hans J. *The Reformation: A Narrative History Related by Contemporary Observers and Participants.* Grand Rapids, MI: Baker, 1978.

Hitchcock, James. *Catholicism and Modernity: Confrontation or Capitulation?* New York: Seabury Press, 1979.

Hoekendijk, Johannes C. *The Church Inside Out.* L.A. Hoedemaker and Pieter Tijmes, eds., Isaac C. Rottenberg, trans. London: SCM, 1966.

Hoffer, Eric. *The Temper of Our Time.* New York: Harper & Row, 1967.

Hostie, Raymond S.J. *The Life and Death of Religious Orders: A Psycho-Sociological Approach.* Washington, DC: Center for Applied Research in the Apostolate, 1983.

Hunter, George G. III. *To Spread the Power: Church Growth in the Wesleyan Spirit.* Nashville: Abingdon Press, 1987.

Hutton, J. E. *A History of the Moravian Church.* 2nd edn. London: Moravian Publication Office, 1909.

Johnson, Andrew. *If I Give My Soul: Faith Behind Bars in Rio de Janeiro.* New York: Oxford University Press, 2017.

King, Bryan. "A Local Church Takes on the Great Commission" [podcast]. *Movements*, December 18, 2017. https://www.movements.net/blog/blog/2017/12/5/151-a-local-church-takes-on-the-great-commission-bryan-king . Accessed December 18, 2017.

Kruse, Colin G. *The Gospel of John: An Introduction and Commentary.* Tyndale New Testament Commentaries. Leicester, UK: InterVarsity Press, 2003.

Kuhn, Thomas S. *The Structure of Scientific Revolutions.* 2nd edn, Chicago, IL: University of Chicago, 1970.

Latourette, Kenneth Scott. *A History of the Expansion of Christianity, Vol. 1: The First Five Centuries.* London: Eyre and Spottiswoode, 1938.

———. *A History of the Expansion of Christianity Vol. 3: Three Centuries of Advance A.D. 1500–A.D. 1800* . London: Eyre and Spottiswoode, 1939.

———. *A History of Christianity, Vol. I: Beginnings to A.D. 1500.* New York: Harper & Row, 1975.

Lehtonen, Risto. *Story of a Storm: The Ecumenical Student Movement in the Turmoil of Revolution, 1968 to 1973.* Publications of the Finnish Society of Church History 174. Grand Rapids, MI: Eerdmans, 1998.

Lipka, Michael. "Mainline Protestants Make up Shrinking Number of U.S. Adults." *Pew Research Center* [blog], May 18, 2015. http://www.pewresearch.org/fact-tank/2015/05/18/mainline-protestants-make-up-shrinking-number-of-u-s-adults/ . Accessed February 27, 2019.

Long, Justin. "The Brutal Facts." *Mission Frontiers* (February 2018).

MacKay, Danny. "164-NoPlaceLeft Canada" [podcast]. *Movements,* June 1, 2018. https://www.movements.net/blog/blog/2018/4/3/163-noplaceleft-canada . Accessed June 18, 2018.

Matson, David Lertis. *Household Conversion Narratives in Acts: Pattern and Interpretation.* Sheffield, UK: Sheffield Academic Press, 1996.

Mauser, Ulrich W. *Christ in the Wilderness: The Wilderness Theme in the Second Gospel and Its Basis in the Biblical Tradition.* Studies in Biblical Theology 39. London: SCM Press, 1963.

Merrill, Eugene H. "Remembering: A Central Theme in Biblical Worship." *Journal of the Evangelical Theological Society* 43/1 (March 2000).

Morris, Leon. *The Biblical Doctrine of Judgment*. London: Tyndale Press, 1960.

———. *The Gospel According to Matthew*. The Pillar New Testament Commentary. Grand Rapids, MI: Eerdmans, 1992.

Nadler, David A. and Mark B. Nadler. "The Success Syndrome: Why Established Market Leaders Usually Stumble—and What You Can Do to Prevent It." *Leader to Leader,* 7 (Winter 1998).

Neill, Stephen. *Creative Tension*. Duff Lectures. Edinburgh: Edinburgh House Press, 1959.

Niebuhr, Richard, H. *The Kingdom of God in America*. New York: Harper & Row, 1959.

Origen. "Against Celsus, III.55." In J. Stevenson ed., *A New Eusebius: Documents Illustrative of the History of the Church to A.D. 337*. London: SPCK, 1960.

Oswalt, John N. *The Book of Isaiah: Chapters 1–39*. The New International Commentary on the Old Testament. Grand Rapids, MI: Eerdmans, 1986.

Peters, Tom. "Rule #3: Leadership is Confusing as Hell." *Fast Company,* 44 (February 2001).

Petersen, Rodney L. "Francis of Assisi and the Franciscan Ideal." In John D. Woodbridge, ed., *Great Leaders of the Christian Church*. Chicago: Moody, 1988.

Pillai, Kumar. "150-Asia to the World" [podcast]. *Movements* (December 4, 2017). https://www.movements.net/blog/blog/2017/12/4/150-asia-to-the-nations-kumar-pillai . Accessed February 21, 2018.

Platt, David. *Radical: Taking Back Your Faith from the American Dream.* Colorado Springs: Multnomah, 2010.

Pollock, John C. *A Cambridge Movement.* London: John Murray, 1953.

Potter, Sarah. "The Making of Missionaries in the Nineteenth Century: Conversion and Convention." In Michael Hill ed., *A Sociological Yearbook of Religion in Britain* 8. London: SCM Press, 1975.

Punshon, John. *Portrait in Grey: Short History of the Quakers.* London: Quaker Home Service, 1984.

Quinn, Robert E. *Deep Change: Discovering the Leader Within.* San Francisco: Jossey-Bass, 1996.

Rack, Henry D. *Reasonable Enthusiast: John Wesley and the Rise of Methodism.* 2nd edn. Nashville, TN: Abingdon Press, 1992.

Roberts, Arthur O. "George Fox and the Quakers." In Tim Dowley ed., *The History of Christianity.* Surry Hills, NSW: Anzea Books, 1977.

Rosner, Brian. "The Progress of the Word." In I. Howard Marshall and David Peterson eds., *Witness to the Gospel: The Theology of Acts.* Grand Rapids: Eerdmans, 1998.

Schnabel, Eckhard J. *Early Christian Mission, Vol. 1: Jesus and the Twelve.* Downers Grove, IL: IVP Academic, 2004.

———. *Early Christian Mission, Vol. 2: Paul And The Early Church.* Downers Grove, IL: IVP Academic, 2004.

———. *Paul the Missionary: Realities, Strategies and Methods.* Downers Grove, IL: IVP Academic, 2008.

Senge, Peter M. *The Fifth Discipline: The Art and Practice of the Learning Organization.* Milsons Point, NSW: Random House, 1990.

Shank, Nathan. "Generational Mapping: Tracking Elements of Church Formation Within CPM's." *Mission Frontiers ,* November-December 2012.

Shank, Nathan and Kari Shank. "The Four Fields Kingdom Growth: Starting and Releasing Healthy Churches." *Movements,* 2014. https://www.movements.net/s/4Fields-of-Kingdom-Growth-Shank-2015-rpw5.pdf . Accessed March 26, 2018.

Shelton, James B. *Mighty in Word & Deed: The Role of the Holy Spirit in Luke-Acts.* Eugene, OR: Wipf and Stock Publishers, 1991.

Sherwood, Harriet. "Justin Welby Unable to Give 'Straight Answer' on Whether Gay Sex Is Sinful." *The Guardian,* October 2, 2017. https://www.theguardian.com/uk-news/2017/oct/02/justin-welby-unable-to-give-straight-answer-on-whether-gay-sex-is-sinful . Accessed November 7, 2017.

Sinek, Simon. *Start with Why: How Great Leaders Inspire Everyone to Take Action.* New York: Portfolio, 2009.

Snyder, Howard A. *The Radical Wesley and Patterns for Church Renewal.* Downers Grove, IL: InterVarsity Press, 1980.

Stark, Rodney. *One True God: Historical Consequences of Monotheism.* Princeton: Princeton University Press, 2003.

———. *The Triumph of Christianity: How the Jesus Movement Became the World's Largest Religion.* New York: Harper Collins, 2011.

Stark, Rodney and Bainbridge, William Sims. *The Future of Religion: Secularization, Revival and Cult Formation.* Berkeley: University of California Press, 1985.

Stein, Robert H. "Baptism and Becoming a Christian in the New Testament." *Southern Baptist Journal of Theology* 2/1 (1998).

Stephenson, Paul. *Constantine: Roman Emperor, Christian Victor.* New York: The Overlook Press, 2009.

Stetzer, Ed, Richard Stanley and Jason Hayes. *Lost and Found: The Younger Unchurched and the Churches That Reach Them.* Nashville, TN: B&H Books, 2009.

Sundell, Jeff, and Angie Sundell. "159-Pioneering NoPlaceLeft in South Asia" [podcast]. *Movements,* March 6, 2018. https://www.movements.net/blog/blog/2018/3/7/159-pioneering-noplaceleft-in-south-asia . Accessed March 29, 2018.

———. "160-Pioneering NoPlaceLeft in the US" [podcast]. *Movements,* April 6, 2018. https://www.movements.net/blog/blog/2018/3/7/160-pioneering-noplaceleft-in-the-us . Accessed April 8, 2018.

Tuchman, Barbara W. *The March of Folly: From Troy to Vietnam.* New York: Random House, 1984.

Vaughn, Ray. "50-On the Frontline with Ray Vaughn" [podcast]. *Movements,* August 13, 2013. https://www.movements.net/blog/2013/08/13/on-the-frontline-with-ray-vaughn.html . Accessed February 21, 2018.

———. "153-Pursuing NoPlaceLeft as a Team" [podcast]. *Movements,* January 13, 2018. https://www.movements.net/blog/blog/2018/1/10/153-pursuing-noplaceleft-as-a-team . Accessed February 21, 2018.

Vaughn, Ray, and Sara Vaughn. "152-Pursuing NoPlaceLeft Together" [podcast]. *Movements*, January 7, 2018. https://www.movements.net/blog/blog/2017/12/5/152-pursuing-noplaceleft-together-ray-sara-vaughn . Accessed February 21, 2018.

Via, Jacob. "131-NoPlaceLeft Haiti" [podcast]. *Movements*, March 5, 2017. https://www.movements.net/blog/2017/2/16/131-noplaceleft-haiti-jacob-via . Accessed February 5, 2018.

Via, Jacob and Marcelin Jephte. "148-Haiti Update from Jacob and Jephte" [podcast]. *Movements*, October 29, 2017. https://www.movements.net/blog/blog/2017/10/16/an-update-from-haiti . Accessed February 5, 2018.

Visser 't Hooft, Willem Adolph. *The Renewal of the Church*. The Dale Lectures. London: SCM Press, 1956.

Walvin, James. *The Quakers: Money and Morals*. London: John Murray, 1997.

Watson, David L. and Paul D. Watson. *Contagious Disciple Making: Leading Others on a Journey of Discovery*. Nashville: Thomas Nelson, 2014.

Waybright, Don. "182-NoPlaceLeft Behind Bars" [podcast]. *Movements*, February 7, 2019. https://www.movements.net/blog/blog/2019/1/21/182-noplaceleft-in-prison . Accessed February 7, 2019.

Wesley, John. *The Complete Works of John Wesley, Vol. 13: Letters, Writings*. Albany, OR: AGES Software, 1996, 1997. https://angletonfumc.org/wp-content/uploads/sites/20/2015/09/Complete-Works-of-John-Wesley-Volume-13.pdf . Accessed March 4, 2019.

———. *The Journal of John Wesley.* http://www.ccel.org/ccel/wesley/journal.html . Accessed August 14, 2017.

Wheatley, Margaret J. *Leadership and the New Science: Learning About Organization From an Orderly Universe.* San Francisco: Berrett-Koehler Publishers, 1994.

White, Justin. "156-Growing Workers for NoPlaceLeft" [podcast]. *Movements,* February 27, 2018. https://www.movements.net/blog/blog/2018/2/25/156-growing-workers-for-noplaceleft . Accessed March 5, 2018.

Wiarda, Timothy. *Spirit and Word: Dual Testimony in Paul, John and Luke.* Library of New Testament Studies 565. London: Bloomsbury, 2017.

Wigger, John H. *Taking Heaven by Storm: Methodism and the Rise of Popular Christianity in America.* Urbana: University of Illinois Press, 1998.

Wright, N. T. *Surprised by Hope: Rethinking Heaven, the Resurrection, and the Mission of the Church.* New York: HarperCollins, 2008.

NOTES

Foreword

[1] Steve Addison, *Movements That Change the World: Five Keys to Spreading the Gospel* (Downers Grove, IL: InterVarsity Press, 2009); *What Jesus Started: Joining the Movement, Changing the World* (Downers Grove, IL: InterVarsity Press, 2012); *Pioneering Movements: Leadership That Multiplies Disciples and Churches* (Downers Grove, IL: InterVarsity Press, 2015).

[2] David Garrison, *A Wind in The House of Islam: How God is Drawing Muslims Around the World to Faith in Jesus Christ* (Monument, CO: WIGTake Resources, 2014); *Church Planting Movements: How God Is Redeeming a Lost World* (Midlothian VA: WIGTake Resources, 2004).

Introduction

[1] See Paul Stephenson, *Constantine: Roman Emperor, Christian Victor* (New York: The Overlook Press, 2009), Kindle Location 2993–3047.

[2] See Richard Fletcher, *The Conversion of Europe: From Paganism to Christianity, 371–1386 AD* (London: Fontana Press, 1997), 19.

[3] Rodney Stark, *One True God: Historical Consequences of Monotheism* (Princeton: Princeton University Press, 2003), 61.

[4] According to Stark, Christianity spread as a network phenomenon through ties of family and friends. The apostles

did not function as settled clergy but traveled widely as the links between networks of congregations that were "run by and recruited by local, part-time amateurs." Stark, *One True God*, 60.

[5] See Rodney Stark, *The Triumph of Christianity: How the Jesus Movement Became the World's Largest Religion* (New York: HarperCollins, 2011), 156.

[6] Kenneth Scott Latourette, *A History of the Expansion of Christianity, Vol. 1: The First Five Centuries* (London: Eyre and Spottiswoode, 1938), 160.

[7] According to Simon Sinek, great leaders begin with *why*—meaning, purpose, and identity. Simon Sinek, *Start with Why: How Great Leaders Inspire Everyone to Take Action* (New York: Portfolio, 2009).

[8] See Eckhard J. Schnabel, *Early Christian Mission, Vol. 1: Jesus and the Twelve* (Downers Grove, IL: IVP Academic, 2004), 95, 355–56.

Chapter 1

[1] In Israel's story the wilderness is a place of both judgment and renewal.

[2] Is 40–55; Mk 10:45. D. A. Carson, "Matthew" in Frank E. Gaebelein, ed., *The Expositor's Bible Commentary, Vol. 8* (Grand Rapids, MI: Zondervan, 1984), 108.

[3] Gen 3:1.

[4] Carson, "Matthew", 113.

[5] In this section I'm indebted to John M. Frame, *The Doctrine of the Word of God* (Phillipsburg, NJ: P & R Publishing, 2010).

[6] See Brian Rosner, "The Progress of the Word," in I. Howard Marshall and David Peterson, eds.,*Witness to the Gospel: The Theology of Acts* (Grand Rapids: Eerdmans, 1998), 215–33.

[7] See Addison, *Pioneering Movements*, 66.

[8] According to Timothy Wiarda, Paul had a similar view of the Word as an active player that "works, runs, comes, bears fruit, grows, dwells and is not bound" (1 Thess 2:13; 2 Thess 3:1; Col 1:4–5; 3:16; 2 Tim 2:9). Through the Word of the gospel "God calls, saves, cleanses and brings people to obedience" (2 Thess 2:14; 1 Cor 1:21; Rom 15:18; Eph 5:26). Timothy Wiarda, "Spirit and Word: Dual Testimony in Paul, John and Luke," *Library of New Testament Studies* 565 (London: Bloomsbury, 2017), 13–14.

[9] Shelton observes, "in Luke–Acts, 'filled with the Holy Spirit' indicates that inspired witness is about to take place." James B. Shelton, *Mighty in Word & Deed: The Role of the Holy Spirit in Luke–Acts* (Eugene, OR: Wipf and Stock Publishers, 1991), 19.

[10] Harry R. Boer, *Pentecost and Missions* (Grand Rapids: Eerdmans, 1961), 161.

[11] Eckhard J. Schnabel, *Paul the Missionary: Realities, Strategies and Methods* (Downers Grove, IL: IVP Academic, 2008), 29. For an excellent discussion on the nature of mission see, Keith Ferdinando, "Mission: A Problem of Definition," *Themelios*, 33/1 (2008), 46–5.

[12] See Addison, *What Jesus Started*.

[13] N. T. Wright provides an example of this shift. He describes what he believes should be at the heart of mission: "... going straight from worshipping Jesus in church to making a radical difference in the material lives of people down the street by running playgroups for children of single working moms; by organizing credit unions to help people at the bottom of the financial ladder find their way to responsible solvency; by campaigning for better housing, against dangerous roads, for drug rehab centers, for wise laws relating

to alcohol, for decent library and sporting facilities, for a thousand other things in which God's sovereign rule extends to hard, concrete reality. Once again, all this is not an extra to the mission of the church. It is central." N.T. Wright, *Surprised by Hope: Rethinking Heaven, the Resurrection, and the Mission of the Church* (New York: HarperCollins, 2008), 267.

[14] Stephen Neill, *Creative Tension*, Duff Lectures (Edinburgh: Edinburgh House Press, 1959), 81.

[15] Robert H. Stein, "Baptism and Becoming a Christian in the New Testament," *Southern Baptist Journal of Theology* 2/1 (1998), 6–17.

[16] Carson, "Matthew," 596.

[17] I've covered the characteristic of Movement Pioneers in two of my previous books: *What Jesus Started* and *Pioneering Movements*. My other book, *Movements That Change the World*, deals with characteristics of Contagious Relationships, Rapid Mobilization, and Adaptive Methods. Readers who are familiar with *Movements That Change the World* will notice that I've reworked the characteristics of *White-hot faith* and *Commitment to the cause* into the essential elements of Word, Spirit, and Mission.

[18] See Addison, *Pioneering Movements*, 65–76.

[19] I wrote in *Pioneering Movements*, "Partnership occurs when local churches and apostolic bands affirm the legitimacy and unique contributions of the other. The pioneers seek out unreached fields. The churches release resources and people for that purpose. The mission band circles back to report to and strengthen existing churches. The churches are responsible for reaching their local areas in depth. They partner with the apostolic band to plant churches in the surrounding regions and beyond. Neither party rules, dominates or controls the other." Addison, *Pioneering Movements*, 72.

[20] Celsus quoted by Origen, "Against Celsus," III.55 in, J. Stevenson, ed., *A New Eusebius: Documents Illustrative of the History of the Church to A.D. 337* (London: SPCK, 1960), 141.

[21] See Eckhard J. Schnabel, *Early Christian Mission, Vol. 2: Paul And The Early Church* (Downers Grove, IL: IVP Academic, 2004), 1425–45.

[22] See Roland Allen, *The Spontaneous Expansion of the Church: and the Causes which hinder it, 3rd ed.* (London: World Dominion Press, 1956). According to Allen, the spontaneous expansion of the church occurs:

- When converts immediately tell their story to those who know them.

- When, from the beginning, evangelism is the work of those within the culture.

- When true doctrine results from the true experience of the power of Christ rather than mere intellectual instruction.

- When the local church is self-supporting and provides for its own leaders and facilities.

- When new churches are given the freedom to learn by experience and are supported but not controlled.

[23] See Tom Peters, "Rule #3: Leadership is Confusing as Hell," *Fast Company,* 44 (February 2001), 124.

[24] A term coined by David A. Nadler and Mark B. Nadler, "The Success Syndrome: Why Established Market Leaders Usually Stumble—and What You Can Do to Prevent It," *Leader to Leader,* 7 (Winter 1998), 43–50.

Chapter 2

[1] Ichak Adizes, *The Pursuit of Prime: Maximize Your Company's Success With the Adizes Program* (Santa Monica, CA: Knowledge Exchange, 1996), 35.

[2] Kenneth Scott Latourette, *A History of Christianity, Vol. 1: Beginnings to A.D. 1500* (New York: Harper & Row, 1975), 428.

[3] Luther P. Gerlach and Virginia H. Hine, *People, Power, Change: Movements of Social Transformation* (Indianapolis: The Bobbs-Merrill Company, 1970), 167.

[4] See Thomas S. Kuhn, *The Structure of Scientific Revolutions*, 2nd ed. (Chicago, IL: University of Chicago Press, 1970), 170.

[5] Bonaventure, a follower and biographer of Francis, quoted in Rodney L. Petersen, "Francis of Assisi and the Franciscan Ideal," in John D Woodbridge, ed., *Great Leaders of the Christian Church* (Chicago: Moody, 1988), 164.

[6] See Jay A. Conger and Rabindra N. Kanungo, "Behavioral Dimensions of Charismatic Leadership," in *Charismatic Leadership: The Elusive Factor in Organizational Effectiveness* (San Francisco: Jossey-Bass, 1988), 7–97.

[7] Sinek, *Start With Why*, 85.

[8] See Addison, *Movements That Change the World*, 15–22, 56–60, 105–106.

[9] Raymond Hostie, *The Life and Death of Religious Orders: A Psycho-Sociological Approach*, English trans. (Washington, DC: Center for Applied Research in the Apostolate, 1983), 109.

Chapter 3

[1] John Wesley. "January 13, 1738," *The Journal of John Wesley.* http://www.ccel.org/ccel/wesley/journal.html, accessed

August 15, 2017. For more on Wesley see Addison, *Movements That Change the World*, 56–64.

[2] Wesley, "May 24, 1738," *The Journal of John Wesley*.

[3] Adizes, *The Pursuit of Prime*, 27.

[4] Ichak Adizes, "Organizational Passages—Diagnosing and Treating Lifecycle Problems of Organizations," *Organizational Dynamics* 8/1 (1979), 6.

[5] John Wesley quoted in Howard A. Snyder, *The Radical Wesley and Patterns for Church Renewal* (Downers Grove IL: InterVarsity Press, 1980), 121.

[6] For Wesley, salvation meant more than deliverance from hell, "By salvation I mean, not barely (according to the vulgar notion) deliverance from hell, or going to heaven, but a present deliverance from sin, a restoration of the soul to its primitive health […] the renewal of our souls after the image of God in righteousness and true holiness, in justice, mercy, and truth". Gerald R. Cragg, ed., *The Works of John Wesley, Vol. 11: The Appeals to Men of Reason and Religion and Certain Related Open Letters* (Nashville, TN: Abingdon Press, 1987), 106.

[7] David Hempton, *Methodism: Empire of the Spirit* (New Haven: Yale University Press, 2005), 78.

[8] Richard P. Heitzenrater, *Wesley and the People Called Methodists*, 2nd ed. (Nashville, TN: Abingdon Press, 1995), 118.

[9] During the class meeting: "inquiry was made into the behavior of every person [. . .] advice or reproof was given as need required, quarrels made up, misunderstandings removed; and after an hour or two spent in this labor of love, they concluded with prayer and thanksgiving." John Wesley quoted in Heitzenrater, *Wesley and the People*, 119.

[10] Heitzenrater, *Wesley and the People*, 176.

[11] Discipline was becoming "the hallmark of the Methodist

movement, with accountability at every level: quarterly ticket-renewal of all members and yearly examination of all preachers and leaders." Heitzenrater, *Wesley and the People,* 176.

[12] Heitzenrater, *Wesley and the People,* 153, 165.

[13] See Heitzenrater, *Wesley and the People,* 147; Henry D. Rack, *Reasonable Enthusiast: John Wesley and the Rise of Methodism,* 2nd ed. (Nashville, TN: Abingdon Press, 1992), 214–18.

[14] See Heitzenrater, *Wesley and the People,* 175–82.

[15] Heitzenrater, *Wesley and the People,* 152.

[16] See Ichak Adizes, *Managing Corporate Lifecycles* (Paramus, NJ: Prentice Hall Press, 1999), 64–70.

[17] See Ichak Adizes, *Corporate Lifecycles: How and Why Corporations Grow and Die and What to Do About It,* 4th ed. (Englewood Cliffs, NJ: Prentice Hall, 1998), 39–41.

[18] See George G. Hunter III, *To Spread the Power: Church Growth in the Wesleyan Spirit* (Nashville: Abingdon Press, 1987), 61.

[19] Adizes, *The Pursuit of Prime,* 27.

[20] Nathan O. Hatch, "The Puzzle of American Methodism," *Church History* 63/2 (June 1994), 178.

[21] Frank Baker, *From Wesley to Asbury: Studies in Early American Methodism* (Durham, NC: Duke University Press, 1976), 116.

[22] John H. Wigger, *Taking Heaven By Storm: Methodism and the Rise of Popular Christianity in America* (Urbana: University of Illinois Press, 1998), 13.

[23] Wigger, *Taking Heaven by Storm,* 4.

Chapter 4

[1] Adizes, "Organizational Passages," 8–9.

[2] For this section I have relied on Walvin's account of Quaker origins and development. See James Walvin, *The Quakers: Money and Morals* (London: John Murray, 1997).

[3] Arthur O. Roberts, "George Fox and the Quakers" in Tim Dowley, ed., *The History of Christianity* (Surry Hills, NSW: Anzea Books, 1977), 480. Fox's followers preferred to be called The Society of Friends, following Jesus' word to his disciples, "Instead I have called you friends" (John 15:13–15).

[4] George Fox, *Autobiography of George Fox*, chapter one. http://www.ccel.org/ccel/fox_g/autobio.pdf , accessed August 16, 2017.

[5] George Fox quoted in Walvin, *The Quakers,* 13–14.

[6] Walvin, *The Quakers*, 19.

[7] Walvin, *The Quakers*, 18.

[8] Walvin, *The Quakers,* 88.

[9] John Punshon, *Portrait in Grey: A Short History of the Quakers* (London: Quaker Home Service, 1984), 113.

[10] Walvin describes how "Businessmen [...] were expected to open their ledgers, show their receipts, reveal their bills and correspondence to satisfy their co-religionists." Walvin, *The Quakers,* 79.

[11] George Fox quoted in William Charles Braithwaite, *The Second Period of Quakerism*, 2nd ed. (Cambridge: Cambridge University Press, 1961), 499.

[12] Walvin, *The Quakers,* 144.

[13] See Adizes, "Organizational Passages," 7.

[14] Peter M. Senge, *The Fifth Discipline: The Art and Practice of the Learning Organization* (Milsons Point, NSW: Random House, 1990), 150.

15 The Old Testament called Israel to remember the words and acts of God (Deut 5:15; 8:2; Ps 77:11; Is 46:8–9). In the New Testament, remembering is associated with the Lord's Supper (Lk 22:19).

16 See Eugene H. Merrill, "Remembering: A Central Theme in Biblical Worship," *Journal of the Evangelical Theological Society* 43/1 (March 2000), 27–36.

17 See Roger Finke, "Innovative Returns to Tradition: Using Core Teachings as the Foundation for Innovative Accommodation," *Journal for the Scientific Study of Religion* 43:1 (March 2004): 19–34.

18 David Lertis Matson, *Household Conversion Narratives in Acts: Pattern and Interpretation* (Sheffield, UK: Sheffield Academic Press, 1996), 124, note 162.

Chapter 5

1 Commonly attributed to Eric Hoffer. Probably adapted from this statement: "What starts out here [in America] as a mass movement ends up as a racket, a cult, or a corporation." Eric Hoffer, *The Temper of Our Time* (New York: Harper & Row, 1967), 51.

2 Barbara W. Tuchman, *The March of Folly: From Troy to Vietnam* (New York: Random House, 1984), 123.

3 Tuchman, *The March of Folly*, 123.

4 Kenneth Scott Latourette, *A History of the Expansion of Christianity, Vol. III, Three Centuries of Advance: A.D. 1500– A.D. 1800* (London: Eyre and Spottiswoode, 1939), 1.

5 Tuchman, *The March of Folly*, 52.

6 See Latourette, *Three Centuries of Advance*, Vol. III, 1.

7 See Latourette, *Three Centuries of Advance*, Vol. III, 7–8.

[8] See Tuchman, *The March of Folly,* 73

[9] Quoted in Tuchman, *The March of Folly,* 61.

[10] Hans J. Hillerbrand, *The Reformation: A Narrative History Related by Contemporary Observers and Participants* (Grand Rapids, MI: Baker, 1978), 19.

[11] Peter Block, *Stewardship: Choosing Service Over Self-Interest* (San Francisco: Berrett-Koehler Publishers, 1993), 147.

[12] Tuchman, *The March of Folly,* 125.

[13] Tuchman, *The March of Folly,* 126.

[14] Quoted in Tuchman, *The March of Folly,* 115.

[15] Gerhard Ebeling, *Luther: An Introduction to His Thought,* trans. R.A. Wilson (London: Collins, 1970), 70.

[16] Ebeling, *Luther,* 66–67.

[17] Edwin Friedman has written extensively on leadership as remaining self-defined with a non-anxious presence. Edwin H. Friedman, *Generation to Generation: Family Process in Church and Synagogue* (New York: The Guilford Press, 1985).

[18] J. Robert Clinton, *Focused Lives: Inspirational Life Changing Lessons From Eight Effective Christian Leaders Who Finished Well* (Altadena: Barnabas Publishers, 1995), 49.

[19] John C. Bennett, *Charles Simeon and the Evangelical Anglican Missionary Movement—A Study of Voluntarism and Church-Mission Tensions,* PhD thesis, University of Edinburgh, 1992, 393–94, quoted in Clinton, *Focused Lives,* 72.

[20] John C. Pollock, *A Cambridge Movement* (London: John Murray, 1953), 7.

Chapter 6

1 See Sarah Potter, "The Making of Missionaries in the Nineteenth Century: Conversion and Convention," in Michael Hill, ed., *A Sociological Yearbook of Religion in Britain 8* (London: SCM Press, 1975), quoted in Steve Bruce, "The Student Christian Movement: A Nineteenth Century Movement and its Vicissitudes," *International Journal of Sociology and Social Policy* 2/1 (1982), 67.

2 Bruce, "The Student Christian Movement," 68.

3 Robin Boyd, *The Witness of the Student Christian Movement: 'Church Ahead of the Church'* (London: SPCK, 2007), 9.

4 Bruce, "The Student Christian Movement," 68–69.

5 Steve Bruce, *Firm in the Faith* (Aldershot, UK: Gower, 1984), 73.

6 Bruce, *Firm in the Faith*, 73.

7 Bruce, *Firm in the Faith*, 83.

8 Bruce, "The Student Christian Movement," 68.

9 Bruce, *Firm in the Faith*, 75–76.

10 Johannes C. Hoekendijk, *The Church Inside Out*, eds., L.A. Hoedemaker and Pieter Tijmes, trans. Isaac C. Rottenberg (London: SCM, 1966), 38.

11 Risto Lehtonen, "Story of a Storm: The Ecumenical Student Movement in the Turmoil of Revolution, 1968 to 1973," *Publications of the Finnish Society of Church History, No 174* (Grand Rapids, MI: Eerdmans, 1998), 25.

12 Lehtonen, *Story of a Storm*, 25.

13 Lehtonen, *Story of a Storm*, 337.

14 Bruce, *Firm in the Faith*, 91. I experienced this first hand as an Australian university student in the mid-1970s. At Monash University, SCM co-hosted lunchtime lectures with the Communist club.

15 Bruce, *Firm in the Faith*, 91.

[16] Lehtonen, *Firm in the Faith,* 332.

[17] Bruce, "The Student Christian Movement," 79.

[18] Bruce, *Firm in the Faith,* 77.

[19] *Student Christian Movement.* https://www.movement.org. uk , accessed May 21, 2001.

[20] Rodney Stark and William Sims Bainbridge, *The Future of Religion: Secularization, Revival, and Cult Formation* (Berkeley: University of California Press, 1985), 429–30.

[21] John N. Oswalt, "The Book of Isaiah Chapters 1–39," *The New International Commentary on the Old Testament* (Grand Rapids, MI: Eerdmans, 1986), 190–91.

[22] See Bruce, *Firm in the Faith,* 70–75.

[23] See Steve Bruce, "The Student Christian Movement and the Inter-Varsity Fellowship: A Sociological Study of Two Student Movements," (University of Stirling, 1980). http://hdl. handle.net/1893/2398 , accessed July 4, 2018.

[24] Addison, *Movements That Change the World,* 63.

[25] Addison, *Movements That Change the World,* 63.

[26] See James Hitchcock, *Catholicism and Modernity: Confrontation or Capitulation?* (New York: Seabury Press, 1979), 19.

[27] See Michael Lipka, "Mainline Protestants Make Up Shrinking Number of U.S. Adults," *Pew Research Center,* [blog], May 18, 2015. http://www.pewresearch.org/fact-tank/2015/05/18/mainline-protestants-make-up-shrinking-number-of-u-s-adults/ , accessed June 18, 2018.

[28] Steve Chalke and Alan Mann, *The Lost Message of Jesus* (Grand Rapids, MI: Zondervan, 2004), 182–83. For a critique of Chalke's views see Mike Gilbart-Smith, "Book Review: The Lost Message of Jesus, by Steve Chalke." https://www.9marks.org/review/lost-message-jesus-steve-chalke , accessed February 27, 2019.

[29] H. Richard Niebuhr, *The Kingdom of God in America* (New York: Harper & Row, 1959), 193.

[30] See Arthur E. Cundell, *Judges and Ruth: An Introduction and Commentary*, in D.J. Wiseman, ed., Tyndale Old Testament Commentaries (London: InterVarsity Press, 1968), 24–25.

Chapter 7

[1] See Leon Morris, *The Biblical Doctrine of Judgment* (London: Tyndale Press, 1960), 44–53.

[2] See G. K. Beale with David H. Campbell, *Revelation: A Shorter Commentary* (Grand Rapids: Eerdmans, 2015), 56.

[3] Beale and Campbell, *Revelation*, 56.

[4] Welby said, "I am having to struggle to be faithful to the tradition, faithful to the scripture, to understand what the call and will of God is in the 21st century and to respond appropriately with an answer for all people – not condemning them, whether I agree with them or not – that covers both sides of the argument. And I haven't got a good answer, and I am not doing that bit of work as well as I would like." Quoted in Harriet Sherwood, "Justin Welby Unable to Give 'Straight Answer' on Whether Gay Sex Is Sinful," *The Guardian*, October 2, 2017. https://www.theguardian.com/uk-news/2017/oct/02/justin-welby-unable-to-give-straight-answer-on-whether-gay-sex-is-sinful , accessed November 7, 2017.

[5] Ruth Gledhill, "Massive Collapse in Number of Anglicans in Britain, New Survey Shows," *Christian Today*, September 4, 2017. https://www.christiantoday.com/article/massive.collapse.in.number.of.anglicans.in.britain.new.survey.shows/113016.htm , accessed November 7, 2017.

[6] Addison, *Movements That Change the World*, 60. See also

Margaret J. Wheatley, *Leadership and the New Science: Learning About Organization From an Orderly Universe* (San Francisco: Berrett-Koehler Publishers, 1994), 18–19.

[7] See Robert E. Quinn, *Deep Change: Discovering the Leader Within* (San Francisco: Jossey-Bass, 1996), 3–5.

[8] Mark J. Boda, "Return to Me: A Biblical Theology of Repentance," in D. A. Carson, ed., *New Studies in Biblical Theology 35* (Downers Grove, IL: InterVarsity Press, 2015), 181.

[9] Boda, "Return to Me," 164.

[10] Boda, "Return to Me," 145–46.

[11] Ps 80:9–16; Is 5:1–7; Ez 15:1–8.

[12] D. A. Carson, "The Gospel According to John," *The Pillar New Testament Commentary* (Grand Rapids MI: Eerdmans, 1991), Kindle Location 10871.

[13] Colin Kruse contends "When Jesus said the disciples were to 'go' and bear fruit, the 'going' most likely refers to their missionary endeavours. The 'fruit' they were to bear in their going would be new believers." Colin G. Kruse, "The Gospel of John: An Introduction and Commentary," *Tyndale New Testament Commentaries* (Leicester, UK: InterVarsity Press, 2003), 322.

[14] William Carey quoted in J. E. Hutton, *A History of the Moravian Church* 2nd ed. (London: Moravian Publication Office, 1909), 129.

[15] For a fuller account of the Rebirth of the Moravian movement see Addison, *Movements That Change the World*, 38–42.

[16] Robert L. Gallagher, "The Integration of Mission Theology and Practice: Zinzendorf and the Early Moravians," *Mission Studies* 25 (2008), 187.

[17] See Addison, *Pioneering Movements*, 65–76.

[18] Gallagher, "The Integration of Mission Theology and Practice," 191–92.

[19] Gallagher, "The Integration of Mission Theology and Practice," 192, 195.

Chapter 8

[1] NoPlaceLeft is one of many coalitions around the world pursuing multiplying disciples and churches. Another important stream is often referred to as DMM (Disciple Making Movements). For more on DMM, see David L. Watson and Paul D. Watson, *Contagious Disciple Making: Leading Others on a Journey of Discovery* (Nashville: Thomas Nelson, 2014).

[2] For more on the five levels of leadership see appendix, 193–194.

[3] Jeff and Angie Sundell, "159-Pioneering NoPlaceLeft in South Asia" [podcast], *Movements* (March 26, 2018). https://www.movements.net/blog/blog/2018/3/7/159-pioneering-noplaceleft-in-south-asia , accessed March 29, 2018.

[4] Discovery Bible Study is a participative, obedience-oriented, method of discipleship. For more on Discover Bible Study see appendix, 188–189.

[5] Jeff Sundell, "160-Pioneering NoPlaceLeft in the US" [podcast], *Movements* (April 6, 2018). https://www.movements.net/blog/blog/2018/3/7/160-pioneering-noplaceleft-in-the-us , accessed April 8, 2018.

[6] Refer to the appendix if you are unfamiliar with some of the terms used, such as the Person of Peace, the Commands of Christ, Discovery Bible Study, 3-Thirds Discipleship, and 4-Fields.

[7] For more on Discovery Bible Study see appendix.

[8] Marcelin Jephte and Jacob Via, "148-Haiti Update From

Jacob and Jephte" [podcast], *Movements* (October 29, 2017). https://www.movements.net/blog/blog/2017/10/16/an-update-from-haiti , accessed February 5, 2018; Jacob Via, "131-Noplaceleft Haiti" [podcast], *Movements* (March 5, 2017). https://www.movements.net/blog/2017/2/16/131-no placeleft-haiti-jacob-via , accessed February 5, 2018.

9 See Troy Cooper, "4Fields Discovery: Gospels and Acts" [video], *Movements*. https://www.movements.net/training-timo thys , accessed March 12, 2018.

10 See Troy Cooper, "Church Circles Discovery: Epistles" [video], *Movements*. https://www.movements.net/training-tim othys , accessed March 12, 2018.

11 For more on the person or household of peace see appendix, 186.

12 See Matson, *Household Conversion Narratives*, 70–75.

13 Danny MacKay, "164-NoPlaceLeft Canada" [podcast], Movements (June 1, 2018). https://www.movements.net/blog/blog/2018/4/3/163-noplaceleft-canada , accessed June 18, 2018.

14 Justin White, "156-Growing Workers for Noplaceleft" [podcast], *Movements* (February 27, 2018). https://www.movements.net/blog/blog/2018/2/25/156-growing-workers-for-noplaceleft , accessed March 5, 2018.

15 See David Platt, *Radical: Taking Back Your Faith from the American Dream* (Colorado Springs: Multnomah, 2010).

16 Bryan King, "151-A Local Church Takes on the Great Commission" [podcast], *Movements* (December 18, 2017). https://www.movements.net/blog/blog/2017/12/5/151-a-local-church-takes-on-the-great-commission-bryan-king , accessed February 21, 2018.

17 Troy Cooper, "112-Churches Pioneering Movements in Tulsa" [podcast], *Movements* (April 10, 2016). https://

www.movements.net/blog/2016/04/10/112-churches-pioneering-movements-in-tulsa-troy-cooper.html , accessed February 21, 2018.

[18] For more on 3-Thirds Discipleship and the Commands of Christ see appendix, 188–189.

[19] Ray Vaughn, "50-on the Frontline with Ray Vaughn" [podcast], *Movements* (August 13, 2018). https://www.movements.net/blog/2013/08/13/on-the-frontline-with-ray-vaughn.html , accessed February 21, 2018.

[20] Ray Vaughn, "50-On the Frontline".

Ray and Sara Vaughn, "152-Pursuing NoPlaceLeft Together" [podcast], *Movements* (January 7, 2018). https://www.movements.net/blog/blog/2017/12/5/152-pursuing-noplaceleft-together-ray-sara-vaughn , accessed February 21, 2018.

Ray Vaughn, Sara Vaughn and Team, "153-Pursuing Noplaceleft as a Team" [podcast], *Movements* (January 13, 2018). https://www.movements.net/blog/blog/2018/1/10/153-pursuing-noplaceleft-as-a-team , accessed February 21, 2018.

[21] See Addison, *Pioneering Movements*, 73–74.

[22] See Ed Stetzer, Richie Stanley, and Jason Hayes, *Lost and Found: The Younger Unchurched and the Churches that Reach Them* (Nashville, TN: B&H Publishing, 2009), 54–55.

[23] Kumar Pillai, "150-Asia to the World" [podcast], *Movements* (December 4, 2017). https://www.movements.net/blog/blog/2017/12/4/150-asia-to-the-nations-kumar-pillai , accessed February 21, 2018. For a more detailed account of Kumar's background see Steve Addison, *Pioneering Movements*, 84–90.

[24] For more on the Commands of Christ see appendix, 188.

[25] Troy Cooper, "Bi-Vocational Weekly Rhythm" [video], *Movements.* https://www.movements.net/training-timothys , accessed February 12, 2018.

[26] A more extensive list of NoPlaceLeft Adaptive Methods is available in the appendix, 186–194.

[27] For more on the 3-Circles see appendix, 187.

[28] For more on 3-Thirds Discipleship see appendix, 189.

[29] See "The Great Commission Pipeline," [including video], *Movements* (April 9, 2018). https://www.movements.net/blog/blog/2018/4/8/the-great-commission-pipeline , accessed April 9, 2018.

Appendix

[1] Nathan and Kari Shank, "The Four Fields of Kingdom Growth: Starting and Releasing Healthy Churches" [video], *Movements,* 2014. https://www.movements.net/4fields , accessed March 26, 2018. I've unpacked the 4-Fields Strategy in my book, *What Jesus Started.*

[2] See "Modelling 411 Training" [video], *Movements.* https://www.movements.net/411 , accessed March 26, 2018.

[3] See Nathan Shank, "Generational Mapping: Tracking Elements of Church Formation Within CPM's," *Mission Frontiers* (November-December 2012), 26–30; and Nathan Shank and Kari Shank, "Four Fields of Kingdom Growth," 93–95.

[4] See Shank, "The Four Fields," 108–115; and Addison, *Pioneering Movements,* 95–108.

ACKNOWLEDGMENTS

I want to thank Dr Robert Clinton, formally of Fuller Seminary, who in the summer of 1990 introduced me to the work of Ichak Adizes on the lifecycle of organizations and that of Gerlach and Hine on the characteristics of movements. Your own writings helped me grasp how God shapes Identity over the course of a leader's life.

Thanks to Sue Davidson, Janet Maxim, Dave Milne, Nathan and Kari Shank, Troy Cooper, Steve Parlato, Buck Rogers, Dave Lawton, and Chuck Wood, for providing input and corrections for the early drafts. Thanks to Grant Morrison, loyal friend and fearless critic.

I've learned that the secret to a good book is good content plus a great editor. This project has had three major edits each by a different editor: first Miriam Ettrick, then Val Gresham, and finally Anna Robinson. You've given me confidence as a writer, you've helped me get my message out, and you've made the experience for our readers so much better. Thank you all.

To Peter Bergmeier, the artist behind the diagrams for each of my four books. I love the simplicity and impact of your designs.

Michelle, thank you for gracefully enduring a husband who has been obsessed with movements for most of our married life!

Finally, this book is dedicated to our four children, Danni, Gretta, Robert, and Lachlan. We love you deeply and we're proud.

STEVE ADDISON is a catalyst for movements that multiply disciples and churches everywhere. He is a missions leader, author, speaker, and mentor to pioneers.

Steve is married to Michelle. They live in Melbourne, Australia and have four children and two grandchildren. Michelle and Steve lead MOVE (movenetwork.org), a mission agency devoted to training and deploying workers who multiply disciples and churches.

Also from Steve Addison

 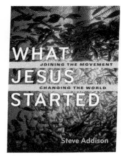 

With a sensitivity to history and an ability to extract principles from the lives of the apostolic pioneers that have gone before us, Steve gives us an inspirational peek into movements and the people who lead them.

ALAN HIRSCH

Discover more

 movements.net

 movements.net

 @movementsnet

Lightning Source UK Ltd.
Milton Keynes UK
UKHW010134140919
349738UK00001B/117/P